# ENGLISH
## Commercial Correspondence
### A First Practice Book

## MICHAEL PAINE

**HARRAP**

London Paris

First published in Great Britain 1991
by HARRAP BOOKS Ltd
Chelsea House, 26 Market Square,
Bromley, Kent BR1 1NA

© Michael Paine 1990

ISBN 0 245 60304-2

Designed by Roger King Graphic Studios.
Printed in Great Britain by
Mackays of Chatham Ltd, Kent.

*To M.I.P.*

# CONTENTS

# INTRODUCTION

*English Commercial Correspondence* is a self-study course for students of English as a Foreign Language who wish to familiarize themselves with the structures and vocabulary used in English business letters. Students using the course should have basic knowledge of English grammar and a vocabulary of about two thousand words. Footnotes are provided to explain purely idiomatic expressions, and all words necessary to understand the letters are highlighted in the text and included in the Glossary. A full key is provided for the comprehension questions and the guided-writing exercises.

The book is divided into four main parts. Part 1 covers twelve introductory subject areas. Each unit is based on four short practice letters which combine to form the material for gap-filling, reordering and guided writing exercises. Thus, by a process of frequent repetition, students assimilate, retain and use the main sentence patterns and vocabulary of English commercial correspondence with very little effort.

Intensive practice on sentence structure is provided in the Drill sections where many more vocabulary items are introduced. The Drills are followed by a Grammar Check which seeks to clarify any grammatical difficulties and provides a general revision of the main grammatical points that occur in the letters.

Part 2 introduces eight more subject areas for further study and practice. The letters in this section are unsimplified and longer than those in Part 1, but students who have worked carefully through the the first twelve Units will have little or no difficulty in completing Part 2.

All the letters appearing in Parts 1 and 2 are consolidated and revised in Part 3. This consists of gap-filler recall exercises that can be checked against the original letters in the units.

The Key provides answers to the comprehension questions and exercises, plus suggested answers for the guided letter-writing exercises. Complete answers are also provided for the drill sections.

On completing the course, students will have studied many different types of letters and will have become thoroughly familiar with the main structural and functional patterns of English business correspondence, such as asking for information, placing orders, complaining about errors and applying for jobs. They will also have gained active control over essential areas, such as general layout, the position of the inside address, the various forms of salutation, etc.

*Objectives*

# To the Student

## The Letters

Note the subject of the Unit, then go to Letter 1. Study the letter, paying particular attention to the new vocabulary and language forms. Try to determine the meaning of any new or difficult words from the context before looking them up in the Glossary. The footnotes will help you with any idiomatic expressions.

Once you have understood the general meaning of the letter, read it through as many times as necessary, until you are satisfied that everything is clear. Next, complete the comprehension questions. To check your answers to the questions, refer to the Key at the end of the book. Work through Letters 2, 3 and 4 in the same way.

## The Drills

The drills provide the chance to practise key structures using new items of vocabulary. In theory these are written exercises, although for fluency practice they can be said aloud, or silently in your head. They deliberately incorporate some long and complex sentences, but again answers can be checked in the key.

## Grammar Check

This section explains the main grammatical points that occur in each unit. Study the explanations and then refer back to the letters and note the use of each point.

## The Exercises

The three exercise types in each unit are based on the structures and vocabulary you have already met in Letters 1—4. Make sure you are familiar with these new language items before attempting the gap-filling test in Exercise 1. Exercise 2 is an exercise on reordering sentences which you will be able to complete provided you have fully understood Letters 1—4. Exercise 3 is a guided writing exercise, with model answers given in the Key. Try to do this exercise on a typewriter or word processor and practise correct layout and punctuation, as described in the appendix.

## The Recall Exercises

The recall exercises for a particular unit should not be attempted immediately after you have completed that unit. Instead, they should be used cyclically. For example, one or two exercises should be attempted for Unit 1 after you have completed Unit 2; a few more after Unit 3, and so on. By using this method, the units are continually revised in a way which assures complete assimilation of the lesson material.

# To the Teacher

Although *English Commercial Correspondence* is designed for self-study, it is also suitable for classroom learning. It can be used as the main course or as a supplementary component of a general course in Business English.

The units are organized so that there is a progression of difficulty throughout the book. However, they can be studied in any order according to the level and the needs of the student. The types of exercise (i.e. completion, reordering and guided-writing) are the same in each of the first twelve units, so that students know exactly what is expected of them. Furthermore, the combining of letters in each unit to form the exercises helps students to develop quickly a familiarity and confidence with the new material. On completion of the first twelve units, students experience the satisfaction of progressing to the eight more advanced units of Part 2, where the model letters and guided-writing exercises are longer.

For use with a class, the following procedures are suggested:

## Aims

Focus on the title and elicit from the students any vocabulary or structures they might already know which are relevant to the letters in the unit.

## Presentation and Comprehension

First, ask students to read the comprehension questions. This focuses their attention on the text and gives them a reason for reading. Next, ask students to read the first letter silently; then read it to the class yourself. Explain any vocabulary and structural difficulties, then ask students to answer the comprehension questions. Check the answers orally and ask further questions. With more advanced students, the comprehension questions can be used as the basis of discussion. In this case, allow students to work in pairs or groups to prepare their answers first.

Repeat this procedure with the four letters in the unit. From time to time, give one of the letters as a dictation.

## Language in Focus

Refer to the Grammar Check section and explain any difficulties. Elicit additional examples from the students. This work can be supplemented by setting further exercises from the relevant sections of the students' general EFL language course book.

## Exercises

Ask students to complete the exercises, working individually or in pairs. Check as many as you can in class, then elicit oral answers from the class as a whole.

*The Recall Exercises*

These are designed to reinforce the letters of each unit at various levels. They focus mainly on new vocabulary but also test knowledge of verb tenses, phrasal verbs and prepositions.

# Pair and Group Work

Except when it is necessary to set an exercise as a test, it is strongly recommended that students work in pairs, and occasionally, in groups. Both the Recall Exercises and the Key can be used as the basis for student-student interaction with students working through the exercises orally and checking each other. On these occasions, the teacher should sit in with the weaker students.

A more advanced class can tackle pair work tasks, e.g.:

Student A writes a letter to a client offering a discount of 25% on a range of convertible armchairs and settees. The letter is then passed to Student B who answers saying the offer is interesting and requesting more details and a price list.

Students can include in their letters the items for sale, company names, letterheads etc., from the book.

A further example of this type of activity might be:

Student A writes a letter to a company saying that the goods they ordered have been shipped by X. Student B replies by complaining that some of the boxes were damaged during transport, and asks the supplier what he intends to do about the problem.

Teachers will find that many of the letters in the course can be adapted in this way.

Michael Paine
Bahrain University, 1991

# PART ONE
## PRACTICE UNITS 1 – 12

# Requests for information

*Study the model letters, answer the questions and complete the exercises.*

*Letter 1.1*

---

## FINEX
### GARDEN PRODUCTS plc [1]
### Agricultural, Horticultural and Forestry Equipment

Finex House, 12-15 Pelham Street, Ilkeston, Lancashire LE7 8AT,
UNITED KINGDOM - Tel: 0906-601536 Tx: 75634 - Fax: 0906 674521

---

Your ref: MG/EJ/ln
Our ref: EJ/MG - 1

4 March 1991

Mr J Godart,
Sales Manager,
AGRICOBEL,
23 avenue Emile Zola,
96453 BOBIGNY
France

Dear Mr Godart,

We **acknowledge\*** reception of your brochure presenting[2]
the new items in your Weedolex range.

We would be very grateful if you would let us have
**further\*** details of your products.

Yours sincerely,

Eric Jones,
Director

[1] public liability company
[2] showing

a) *What did Mr Godart send to Eric Jones?*
b) *What further information does Eric Jones want Mr Godart to send?*

*Letter 1.2*

Dear Mr Jones,

We have been **particularly*** attracted by the steering-wheel locks, model X3/27 on page 43 of your brochure.

Could you possibly let us know if you are in a position[3] to deliver direct?

Yours sincerely,

Patrick Littlejohn,
Chief Buyer

[3] able to / can

a) *Where did Mr Littlejohn find out about the steering-wheel locks?*
b) *What is the purpose of this letter?*
c) *What suggests that the two men have done business with each other?*

*Letter 1.3*

Dear Sirs,

We were very interested to receive your letter of 8th
June announcing the **launching\*** of your new hydraulic
**jacks\***.

Could you possibly send us the address of the
**distributor\*** for our area?

Yours faithfully,


Jack Rothwell,
Manager

a) *What was the purpose of the letter that Mr Rothwell received on
   8 June?*
b) *Does he intend to buy direct from the factory?*

*Letter 1.4*

Dear Sirs,

We would like to add your special range of coats to our
silk and woollens business.

We would be grateful if you would send us your **current\***
price list and let us know your conditions for delivery
**overseas\***.

Yours faithfully,


Janet Watkins,
Overseas Sales Manager

a) *How does Janet Watkins intend to expand her range of goods?*
b) *What further details does she require?*
c) *What is her position in the company?*

# Drills

*Complete the sentences as in the examples. Make changes where necessary:*

1) We / acknowledge reception of your / letter on / 9th January / presenting / your new / range of ski boots.

   a) I / brochure / 10th August / prices.
   b) We / delivery **schedules*** / 8 February / enlarged network.
   c) The directors / **draft*** plans / 21 March / modernization project.
   d) Our client / **software*** / 30 November / new filing system.

2) We / would be very grateful if / you would let us have / a revised contract.
   We / would be very much obliged if / you would let us have / some samples.

   a) Our clients / grateful / a statement of account.
   b) We / obliged / an updated price list.
   c) I / grateful / any special requests.
   d) Mr Jackson / obliged / a **pro forma*** invoice.

3) The contents of your letter / have attracted / our / attention and / we / are particularly interested in / Model X3-27 / presented on page / 43.

   a) Your **circular*** / my / tool kits / 54.
   b) Your **leaflets*** / Mrs Field / sports clothes / 72.
   c) Your up-to-date list / my / price changes / 44.
   d) The brochure / Mr Clarke / range of dinner services / 67.

# Grammar Check

1) Letters 1.1, 1.4, Drill 2 - **If.....would**: Normally we do not use **would** in the **if** part of the sentence. However, in business letters, **If.....would** is used when we want to ask someone formally to do something. There are many examples of this use of **would** in the following units.

2) Letters 1.1 and 1.2 - **let + infinitive without to**: **Could you possibly let us have....** **Make** also has the infinitive without **to**, as in **He made me work hard.** But in the passive **make** takes an infinitive **with** to, e.g. **I was made to work hard.**

*Exercise 1.1*

*Complete the following letter informing suppliers that you would like to stock their range of blow moulding machines. In addition, you would like more details and an up-to-date price list. You would also like to know whether it is possible to deliver direct from the factory.*

Dear Sirs,

We ......... ......... of your brochure and we

would like add to ......... ......... .........

......... your ......... of......... .........

......... . ......... ......... ......... .........

......... ......... if you ......... .........

......... further details ......... .........

......... as well as ......... ......... .........

......... ......... . In addition, would it

......... ......... ......... ......... .........

if you could ......... ......... .

Yours ........,

*Exercise 1.2*

*Reorder the following to make a letter similar to Letters 1.1 - 1.4:*

```
Dear Sirs, I acknowledge reception of your
```

```
I would be obliged if you could let me
```

```
overseas delivery. Yours faithfully, ...
```

```
interested in your new
```

```
letter of 9 January and I am particularly
```

```
have your latest price list as
```

```
range of windbreaker jackets.
```

```
well as your conditions for
```

*Exercise 1.3*

*Write a letter from J. Mills, the Director of Dexter's Ltd, Maylands Street, Hemel Hempstead, Herts, HP2 7TF, UK, to Philip Filby, the Director of Intersync plc, 340/345 Goswell Street, London EC1V 7EE. Include the date, references and :*

- mention that you have received their letter of 9 January.
- mention also that you are very interested in their new range of toothbrushes.
- ask if they would be kind enough to let you know their current prices and the name and address of a distributor near you.

# Acknowledging an enquiry

*Study the model letters, answer the questions and complete the exercises.*

*Letter 2.1*

---

**FISCH MEDICAL** Optical Measuring Instruments

College House, Hallen Street, London EC4 3JJ
Managing Director: J. T. Douglas

```
Mrs. F. Schwartzkopf,
F.L. & G.M. Instruments,
1411 N. Laloma Way,
Santa Barbara,
76342 California,
USA                              9 August 1990

Our ref: ML/nh/321

Dear Madam,

Re: Your letter of 5/8/90

Following your request, please find enclosed an
illustrated folder presenting our SELTEK range. In
anticipation[1] of receiving your order, we remain[2],

Yours faithfully,
```

*Jack Kenyon,*

```
Jack Kenyon,
Export Sales Manager

Enc [3]
```

[1] while we are waiting for...
[2] are always
[3] Enclosures

*a)  Who sent the letter referred to in the 'subject line'?*
*b)  What, in this case, does 'Enc' refer to?*
*c)  What kinds of things do Fisch Medical produce?*

Letter 2.2

Dear Mr Bronson,

With reference to your letter of 25th January 19 —, we
have pleasure in sending you our latest catalogue.

We are quite willing to send you all further
**supplementary\*** information. We thank you for your
interest.

Yours  sincerely,


Frederick  Page,
Overseas  Sales  Manager

*a)  What was the purpose of the letter Mr Page received on 25th
January?*
*b)  What suggests that two men know each other?*

*Letter 2.3*

---

Dear Madam,

We thank you very much for your interest in our Purtex
range – aluminium[1] **trays\*** for **bulk\* catering\*** and frozen
food – sizes A1 & A5.

Our representative will supply you with all
supplementary information and will advise you on the
types of trays that will suit your particular
**requirements\***.

Yours faithfully,


Gordon Williams.
Manager

---

[1] Note that the American spelling is aluminum.


a) *What are A1 and A5?*
b) *What sort of business do you think the client has?*
c) *How do you know that Mr Williams places particular value on this*
   *enquiry?*

*Letter 2.4*

---

Dear Sirs,

We have received your letter of 10 August in which you
request details of our range of bottles, boxes and
wide-necked containers for the packaging of food
products, medicines and toiletries.

Please find enclosed our latest catalogue as well as a
list of prices currently in force[2].

We look forward to receiving your order in the very
near future.

Yours faithfully,


John Holmes,
Director – Sarrabia Group

---

¹ now being used

a)  *What was the purpose of the letter written on 10 August?*
b)  *What kind of goods does the Sarrabia Group manufacture?*
c)  *In addition to the catalogue, what else is enclosed?*
d)  *What letters would you expect to find at the bottom of the page?*

## Drills

*Complete the sentences as in the examples. Make changes where necessary :*

1) Following / your / request, / please find enclosed / an up-to-date list.

   a)  Mr Norman's letter / an updated **quotation***.
   b)  my / inquiry / my **outline* proposals***.
   c)  our / request / an application form.
   d)  my / 'phone call / details of the orders **outstanding***.

2) With reference to your letter of / 24 March, / we / have pleasure in sending you / details of our garaging fees.

   a)  4 April / I / the building permit.
   b)  6 February / the partners / an introductory offer.
   c)  13 August / the Customers' Accounts Department / a statement.
   d)  28 June / the company / a credit note.

3) Please find enclosed / details of our special reductions / as well as / the names of three companies in our area.

   a)  our proposed conditions / an outline contract.
   b)  an order form / samples of our pocket files.
   c)  the plans / a **preliminary*** agreement.
   d)  our free coloured brochure / a few samples of our pull-out folders.

## Grammar Check

1) Letter 2.1: **-ing** clauses. When the **-ing** clause is used to say why someone did something, it usually comes first, e.g. **Following your request....** When it takes the place of a relative clause (e.g. **a folder which presents**) it comes after the noun: **an illustrated folder presenting our SELTEK range**. The -ing form is also used if a verb comes after a preposition, e.g. **in anticipation of receiving your order.** See also Letter 2.2, **...in sending....**

*Exercise 2.1*

*Complete the following letter from a supplier to a client acknowledging his letter, and informing him that the Sales Manager will be sending him full information and a current price list.*

```
Dear Mr Smith,


We ........  ........  ........  ........


........  ........ 5th March. Our........


........  ........  ........  ........  ........


you ........  ........  ........ information as


well as ........  ........  ........  ........


........ in force. We look ........  ........


........  ........ order ........  ........


........ future.

Yours ........, John Birchfield - Manager
```

*Exercise 2.2*

*Rewrite the following to form a letter similar to Letters 2.1 - 2.4:*

> we remain, Yours faithfully, ...

> are quite willing to send you

> In anticipation of receiving your order,

> Dear Mr Skinner, We thank you for

```
 ⌐ all supplementary information. ⌐
 ⌐ your interest in our software. We ⌐
```

*Exercise 2.3*

*Write a letter from Mr Chapman of MK Services, Newlands, Hammersmith, London, W6 8BX, to Mr Philips of Freightflight Ltd, Hind Street, Lenham, Maidstone, Kent M17 2LH. Include the date and references and mention that there are enclosures.*

- say that in reply to their letter of 13 May you are sending them your most up-to-date samples.
- mention that they will also find enclosed your latest price list.
- end by saying that you are waiting to receive their order.

*Study the model letters, answer the questions and complete the exercises.*

*Letter 3.1*

---

# TUASNE (Ilkeston) Ltd
## *Super Abrasives**

Gransham House, 3-6 Lewes Street, Ilkeston Derbyshire DE7 8AR

```
Gutierrez Vicen (Javier)
Gutierrez, S.A.
Ecuador, 46
08975 Barcelona
Spain

23rd December 1990

Your ref: T/UK
Our ref: HP/jw


Dear Sirs,

After having examined your brochure presenting your
water-cooled circular* saws, we would like to place an
order for:

100 Code No: 900 54000 diameter thickness 230 mm,
cutting thickness 2.2 mm

250 Code No: 900 54200 diameter thickness 300 mm,
cutting thickness 3.2 mm
Hoping that this will mark the beginning of a
continuing relationship* between our two companies, we
remain,

Yours faithfully,
```

*Henry Pierce*
Henry Pierce
Export Manager

a) *What does the Gutierrez company produce?*
b) *How do you know that the two companies have never done business together before?*

Letter 3.2

Dear Mr Collins,

After having examined the catalogue you recently sent
us, we have pleasure in sending you **herewith\*** an order
for trouser skirts, length 95 cm, on a straight belt
mounting with slide and buttons.

50 maroon, sizes 36, 38, 40
50 black, sizes 42, 44, 46

Please send the shipment by air.

Yours sincerely,

John Wilkins

a) *How do you know that the two companies have done business together before?*
b) *Is Mr Wilkins in a hurry for the order to be delivered?*

*Letter 3.3*

Dear Sirs,

We have received your letter of 5th December. We now
have the pleasure of sending you the enclosed order for
30 pairs of step **ladders*** with top platforms, aluminium
steps and a supporting **strap*** in the open position.
Reference:32.145:

```
10 Height  85cm/4 steps/3   kg
10   "     110cm/5   "  /3.5 kg
10   "     175cm/8   "  /5.5 kg
```

Please arrange delivery by train.

Yours faithfully,


George Pattison,
Chief Buyer

a) *What kind of shop do you think Mr. Pattison has?*
b) *Where might they have to go to pick up the package?*

*Letter 3.4*

Dear Mr Simpson,

Following our telephone conversation of 10 May last, we
are ordering:

15 non-return **valves*** and 10 automatic regulator taps -
DN 10-250 , series 6000-4500.

Please send the goods by normal cargo service.

Hoping that you will **expedite*** the order with your
usual care, I remain,

Yours sincerely,


Freddy Macdonald

a) How does Mr Macdonald know that the goods he wants are in stock?
b) How does he want the goods sent?
c) How do you know that he feels he can rely on his supplier?

## Drills

*Complete the sentences as in the examples. Make changes where necessary:*

1) After having examined the / brochure presenting your merchandise, / we would like to place an order for / 100 extra-fine-quality, white, poplin shirts @ £25.

   a) catalogue / I / 50 table services, model Savoy.
   b) circular / we / 150 shoe **racks\*** - size 57 x 21 cm.
   c) brochure / I / 30 Multi-Spark electric gas lighters.
   d) leaflet / we / order / 20 9V digital kitchen **scales\***.

2) After having examined the / catalogue / you sent us, / we /have the pleasure of sending you herewith an order for a / Moulinex Master mixer with a juice extractor **attachment\***.

   a) list / me / 20 super compact sewing machines.
   b) samples / us / 5 programmable automatic clothes driers.
   c) brochure / me / 35 rolls of wall-to-wall carpeting.
   d) catalogue / us / 24 Mandi colour televisions (for UK and Continental channels).

3) We / now have pleasure in sending you the enclosed order for / 200 **goose\***-feather continental **quilts\***.

   a) I / a Bontempi portable electronic organ.
   b) We / 10 **collapsible\*** Bak-Pak baby carriers with attached wheels.
   c) Mr. Jackson / 20 Bobby dolls in vinyl, height 40 cm, with closing eyes in the **reclined\*** position.
   d) They / 20 computer disk drives DD1-2, with software.

## Grammar Check

1) Letter 3.1 and 3.1: **After having received....** When one action comes before another action, you can use **having (done)** for the first action.You can also say **After receiving...** but in the more formal style of commercial correspondence the first example is more acceptable.

2) Note also the 'contact clause': **After having examined the catalogue (which) you recently sent us...**, where **which** is

optional. The rule is that when **who** or **that** are the objects of the verb, you can leave them out. An easier way to remember this is, When **who** or **that** are followed by a noun or a pronoun, you can leave them out.

3) Compare the two constructions, **We have pleasure in sending....** and **We have the pleasure of sending....**

*Exercise 3.1*

*Complete the following letter from a client to a supplier placing an order for 100 ignition\* coils\* to be sent by air.*

Dear Sirs,

After ......... ......... ......... brochure

......... ......... ......... us, we.........

......... ......... ......... ......... you

......... ......... ......... 100 ignition coils

CX143/2. ......... ......... shipment by air.

Hoping ......... ......... ......... mark

......... ......... ......... ......... .........

relationship ......... ......... .........

companies, I ......... ,

Yours ........., Martin Lemmon

*Exercise 3.2*

*Reorder the following to make a letter similar to Letters 3.1.- 3.4:*

```
delivery by rail. Hoping that
```

```
you will expedite the order with your
```

```
products, we have pleasure
```

```
in sending you an order for 100
```

```
the samples presenting your
```

```
hypodermic syringes. Please arrange
```

```
usual care, I remain,
```

```
Yours faithfully, Philip Latour.
```

```
Dear Mr Hornby, After having examined
```

*Exercise 3.3*

*Write a letter from Marcus Emmett, the Chief Buyer of Techtronics plc, 56 Calton Street, London EC4N 5AB, UK (Tel: 01-345 335 Telex: 98723, Fax: 01-345 0453) to Electro Inc., Fasanenstr 34, 1000 Berlin 16, Germany. Include the date and references, and mention that:*

- you received his letter of 5th June.
- you have examined their catalogue.
- you include an order number 234/X42 for 200 mechanical **gaskets\***.
- you would like the goods sent by air.
- end the letter appropriately.

# Dealing with orders

*Study the model letters, answer the questions and complete the exercises.*

*Letter 4.1*

## ELEXENCE
### Continental Foodstuffs

Milton Road,
Exeter,
Devon Ex5 6JR
Tel: 0392-56438
Telex: 43532

```
Forrest Foods (Delicatess plc)
49 Woodbridge Road
Paignton
Devon TQ3 3BJ

21 June 19..
Our ref: EA/214
Your ref:
```

```
Dear Sirs,

We thank you for your order No. 321/4-9 for:

- 200 kg of Kenya 1 (coffee) quality No: 493 @ £4.50 kg
- 150 kg of Extra 2 (coffee) quality No: 365 @ £4.65 kg

The goods will be sent today by rail.


Yours faithfully,
```

*Dave Burbridge.*

```
Dave Burbridge
Sales Manager
```

a) *What is the name of the Forrest Foods parent company?*
b) *What sort of a company do you think it is?*
c) *When does the writer say the goods will be sent?*

*Letter 4.2*

Dear Sirs,

Thank you for your letter of 4th November and for the
**accompanying\*** order.

We will let you know when we will be able to **confirm\***
shipment of the goods.

We thank you once more for your order.

Yours faithfully,


Thomas Hamilton
Sales Manager

a) *What was included in the letter written on 4 November?*
b) *Why will Mr Hamilton soon be writing to his client again?*

*Letter 4.3*

Dear Sirs,

I have pleasure in acknowledging receipt of your order
of the 15th **instant\*** regarding:

- the aluminium sheeting
- the polyethylene **laminate\***

We have all the articles in stock and everything should
be ready for shipment next week.

Yours faithfully,

Greg Dodgson
Sales Manager

a) *When will Mr Dodgson be able to send the order?*

*Letter 4.4*

```
Dear Madam,

We are happy to inform you that your order No. 264/3613
of 6 June is in hand¹.

The packets will arrive before the end of the month. We
would be grateful* if you would inform us when the
goods arrive.

Hoping that this arrangement is acceptable, we remain,

Yours faithfully,


Harold Fielding
Export Department
```

¹ is being dealt with

a) *When will the goods arrive?*
b) *What is the arrangement Mr Fielding refers to in the last sentence?*

# Drills

*Complete the sentences as in the examples. Make changes where necessary:*

1) We / have pleasure in acknowledging your order of the /
   12th / instant  regarding the / MF/2DD double sided, double
   density 3½" micro floppy disks.

   a) I / 15th / computer game joy-sticks.
   b) The Sales Department / 6th / typewriters "Eurotype".
   c) Mr Collins / 12th / tailored, 100% cotton, velvet skirts.
   d) We / 18th / short-sleeved, **striped\* polo-necked\*** pullovers.

2) The goods / will be sent / tomorrow / by plane.

   a)  everything / today / train.

   b)  packets / at the end of the week / ship.
   c)  container / tomorrow / road.
   d)  goods / at the end of the month / air.

3) We / have the / shoes / in stock and everything should be ready for shipment / on 7 May.

   a)  I / **overalls\*** / very soon.
   b)  We / cupboards / in a week's time.
   c)  Our shop / quilts / as soon as possible.
   d)  Our branch / **sanding\*** machines / within a few days.

## *Grammar Check*

1) Note the use of **will** to predict a future happening. In Letter 4.1 **The goods will be sent today by rail** does not express a possibility or intention, but says what we are sure will happen. Other examples are **We will let you know...** and **We will be able to confirm...** in Letter 4.2, and **The packets will arrive...** in Letter 4.4.

2) **Should** in **Everything should be ready for shipment...** in Letter 4.3 has the same meaning as **ought to** and must not be confused with the use of **would** in **We would be grateful if you would...** in Letter 4.4. For this use of **would** see Unit 1.

*Exercise 4.1*

*Complete the following letter from a supplier to a client thanking him for his order of 10,000 dustbin-liners in pre-cut rolls and 1000 freezer bags.*

Dear Sirs,

We .........  .........  .........  .........

.........  .........  ......... 435/23/32, for

.........  .........  .........  .........  .........

......... ......... ......... ......... .........

We ......... ......... ......... ......... in

stock, and everything ......... ......... .........

......... ......... within a very few days. The

goods ......... ......... ......... .........

train.  Hoping ......... ......... .........

......... acceptable, we remain,

Yours faithfully,


*Exercise 4.2*

*Rewrite the following to produce a letter similar to Letters 4.1 - 4.4.*

is acceptable, we remain,

letter of 7th March and for the accompanying

before the end of next week.

Dear Sirs, We thank you for your

Yours faithfully, James Harrison.

Hoping that this arrangement

order. The containers will arrive

## Exercise 4.3

*Write a letter from Richard Watson, the Sales Manager of T.I. & E.R.,
65-67 Spencer Street, Ramsgate, Kent, CT11 9LD (Tel: 0856-89674,
Telex: 90867534), who deal in polyethylene sheeting, to Beta Mesures
ETS, France, 54, rue d' Aguesseau, Post Box Number 43, 93190 Noisy-
le-Sec CEDEX. Mention that:*

- you received their order of 12 September for 6 large
  **tarpaulins*** for use as covers in buildings under
  construction[1], and 20 plastic agricultural sheets for
  **mulching*** purposes.
- the delivery will take place as soon as possible.
- you would be grateful if they would let you know when
  the goods arrive.
- end the letter appropriately.

[1] being built

# Packing and transport

*Study the model letters, answer the questions and complete the exercises.*

**Letter 5.1**

## ALUFEX UK

South Star Gardens
Swindon
Wilts. SN2 IEU
UK
Tel: 0793-65423
Telex: 0793-78654

Walter Konzern
Lönsstr. 9
Postfach 80675
8000 Leipzig 80
Germany

12 March 19..

Your ref: ALU/34A
Our ref: CH/jl

Dear Sirs,

Following our order No. A/9753 of 5th February, we have
to point out[1] that the 20 sets of triple mirrors 140 -
EQUINOXE 8490 must be delivered with internal lighting,
plugs and switches to our Hull branch.

On the other hand[2], order No. 867/343 must be sent to
our **warehouse\*** in Bremen.

The mirrors should be in **bales\*** covered in **sacking\***
with metal **strapping\***.

In expectation of[3] your future orders to which we shall
always give the greatest care, we remain,

Yours faithfully,

Charles Hillis
General Manager

[1] draw your attention to the fact, indicate
[2] however
[3] hoping for, waiting for

a)  *Is this letter from a client to a supplier or vice versa?*
b)  *What kind of mirror do you think Mr Hillis is referring to?*
c)  *Where must order No. 867/343 be sent?*
d)  *How would Mr Hillis like the second item to be packed?*

*Letter 5.2*

Dear Sirs,

We have received your letter of 5th January.

All the containers are clearly marked with the
**accepted\*** international sign - **fragile\*** - top - bottom.

We thank you for your order.

Yours faithfully,


Gordon Barnes
Director of Overseas Sales

a)  *Who is this letter to, a client or a supplier?*
b)  *What does he say about the packing?*

*Letter 5.3*

Dear Sirs,

Following your letter of 8th August, please find
enclosed the details **concerning\*** the **shipment\*** of our
order No. A/765.

Each article must be packed in special cases to avoid
all risk of damage during transport.

Please deliver the goods to our shipper's **warehouse\***
and send the **invoice\*** in **duplicate\***.

Yours faithfully,


Jill Evans

a)  *Who is this letter from, a client or a supplier?*
b)  *What was the purpose of the letter that Ms Evans received on*
    *8 August?*
c)  *What do you think the shipper will do with the goods?*

*Letter 5.4*

Dear Madam,

As you requested in your letter of 8th March, we are
sending you twenty 50 kg cases of **edible\*** snails by
refrigerated container to Boulogne from the port of
Dover.

We hope that they will arrive quickly and in good
condition, that you will appreciate the quality of our
products and that we shall have the chance to do
business with you again.

Yours faithfully,


Gerald Moss, Director

a) *What was the purpose of the letter written on 8 March?*
b) *How can you tell that Mr Moss is particularly keen to please these customers?*

# Drills

*Complete the sentences as in the examples. Make changes where necessary:*

1) Following our order of / 8th August, we / have to point out that the / lamps (**rustic*** style) / must be delivered to our / Milan branch.

   a) 9 September / I / dressing gowns (with **shawl*** collars) / warehouse in Newhaven.
   b) 5 May / the manager / glass bookcase style Louis XV / office in Berlin.
   c) 6 June / we / childrens' ski suits / Paris branch.
   d) 15 October / we / zodiac sign quartz watches / agency in Berne.

2) The toys / will be shipped / to your shop in Hastings / tomorrow / according to your instructions.

   a) musical **mobiles*** for baby's cots / warehouse in Croydon   / soon
   b) radio-alarm clocks / office in Amsterdam / next week.
   c) cellular telephones TD 8734 / branch in Jena / at the end of the month
   d) shower curtains / depot in Paris / today

3) As / you / requested in your letter of 6 June, / we are sending you the kitchen stove **extractor*** **hoods*** by air from Gatwick airport to Budapest.

   a) the manageress / 9th October / woollen carpets / sea / port of Tilbury / the Hook of Holland.
   b) our manager / 7th August / the compact washing-up machines / rail / Victoria / Lyon.
   c) they / 15th March / garage swing doors / road / Birmingham / Ramsgate.
   d) our customers / 3rd July / pull-down **loft*** stairs / air freight / Heathrow / Prague.

# Grammar Check

1) Note the use of the passive infinitive after **must, should** and
   **will** in Letter 5.1: **must be delivered, must be sent**. The
   passive infinitive is used after all modal verbs, plus **going to,
   want to** and **have to**.

2) Note also the passive of the simple present in Letter 5.2: **are
   marked**. This is formed with the present tense of **to be** and the
   past participle. We use the passive when it is not  very
   important that we should know who did the action.

### Exercise 5.1

*Complete the following letter from a supplier to a client concerning a
delivery of 20 plant* **tubs***\*.*

```
Dear Mr Granger,


Following ........ ......... No. 87430 of 12

January, we ........ ......... ......... .........

that ........ ......... ......... ......... be

......... ......... ......... depot in Southampton.

All ........ containers must ......... .........

......... ......... ......... ......... .........

sign - fragile - top - bottom. We thank ........

......... ......... .........

Yours ........,

Henry Blackstone,
General Manager
```

*Exercise 5.2*

*Reorder the following to create a letter similar to those in 5.1 - 5.4:*

> you again. Yours faithfully, Harry Hall.

> in Exeter. Hoping that you

> products and that we shall have

> be packed in bales

> will appreciate the quality of our

> of 9 January. The boxes will

> the chance to do business with

> Dear Sir, We have received your letter

> and will be shipped to our depot

> covered in sacking with metal strapping

*Exercise 5.3*

Write a letter from Alba Plastics 10, Carlisle Street, Newcastle upon Tyne, NE1 6XE, UK. Tel: 091-786548, Fax: 419 6754 to Groupe Sarrabia, Miguel Angel, 42 - 50, 2875 Madrid, Spain.

- include the date and references.
- say that you are sending the shipping details in reply to their letter of 5th August.
- mention that the goods will be sent, as instructed, by road to their warehouse in Madrid as soon as possible.
- add that you hope that they will arrive quickly and in good condition.
- end by saying that you hope they will appreciate the quality of your products and that you will have a chance to do business with them again.

# Confirmation of delivery

*Study the model letters, answer the questions and complete the exercises.*

*Letter 6.1*

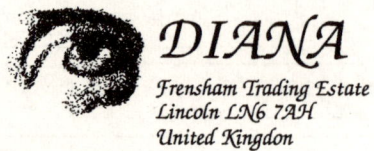

**DIANA**
*Frensham Trading Estate
Lincoln LN6 7AH
United Kingdon*

Your ref: SSP/4/6
Our ref: FIL/2

Martin Lemke
Produkt Forum GmbH
Hindenburgstraße 5-9
Postfach 10 50 60
5000 Köln 50

5 February, 19..

Re: Our order No: 4264/10
Sunscreen Maximal
Coconut-butter Suntan Lotion

Dear Mr Lemke,

We have received the **trial order\*** consisting of the
above-mentioned articles which arrived in perfect
condition.

If, as we hope, our customers like your suntan
products, we shall be pleased to order larger amounts
from you.

Yours faithfully,

James Willis
Managing Director

*Tel: 0522-76549 Telex: 56843 Fax: 0522-51325*

a) *Do you think that SSP have their establishment in the centre of Lincoln?*
b) *What was the purpose of this letter?*
c) *Will Mr Willis place any more orders with Produkt Forum?*

*Letter 6.2*

Dear Sirs,

We thank you for your **consignment\*** of 26 June which arrived this morning within the **required** time and in good condition.

The invoice and the goods **tally\*** perfectly. We hope to be in a position[1] to send you an **identical\*** order **shortly\***.

Yours faithfully,


Janice Green
Director

[1] We hope we can...

a) *How do you know that Janice Green is in a hurry for the goods?*
b) *What came with the goods?*
c) *Is she going to re-order?*

*Letter 6.3*

Dear Sirs,

We are happy to **confirm\*** the arrival of after-shave
lotions Samarkand (No. 1) and Jamaïque (No. 3) which we
ordered two weeks ago (Nos. 210 & 211 of our order No:
3692).

Our lorry collected the goods from the docks yesterday.

In anticipation of the items which have yet to be
delivered, we remain,

Yours faithfully,


Sylvia Witty
Sales Director

a)  *How long has Ms Witty had to wait for this order to arrive?*
b)  *How was it sent?*
c)  *Has she received all of the goods she ordered?*

*Letter 6.4*

Order No. 78654:
<u>50 hanging cupboards 8235: right-hand **hinges\***</u>

Dear Madam,

The first part of the consignment of wall cupboards has
just arrived by rail.

We are happy to confirm that the first **batch\*** delivered
**corresponds\*** perfectly with the delivery note.

You can expect a similar order from us shortly.

Yours faithfully,


John Reynolds
Import Manager

a) *How did the goods arrive?*
b) *How did Mr. Reynolds make sure that everything was in order?*
c) *What does 'batch' refer to?*

# Drills

*Complete the following sentences as in the example. Make changes where necessary.*

1) We have received / the trial order / consisting of the / above-mentioned articles / which arrived in perfect condition.

   a) I / order No: 123A / the bathroom cupboards
   b) Our Brighton branch / the trial order / quilt covers
   c) They / order No. A952 / pure cotton Texas jeans
   d) The shipping company / order No. 43587 / air conditioners

2) We / are happy to confirm the arrival of / the jersey short sleeved pullovers / which we ordered two weeks ago.

   a) I / **windcheaters*** / last month.
   b) Our manager / Eurosport ping-pong tables / a week ago.
   c) Our client / **dressers*** (width 100 cm : height 79 cm) / in January.
   d) Our clients / multi-purpose storage bags / 12 September

3) Our lorry / collected the / goods / from the / docks / yesterday.

   a) Our agent / electric drill attachments / airport / yesterday
   b) My lorry / aerobic **outfits*** / port of Tilbury / tomorrow morning.
   c) My assistant / electric soldering irons / warehouse / next week.
   d) Our customers / **chandeliers*** / storerooms / two days ago

# Grammar Check

1) Note the use of the relative pronoun **which** in Letters 6.1, 6.2 & 6.3: **articles which arrived..., consignment of 26 June which arrived...** and **the after-shave lotions...which we ordered....** In these sentences **that** could also be used instead of **which.**

2) The simple past tense is almost always used when an actual

date or time is given for something, e.g. in Letter 6.2: **We thank you for your consignment of 26 June which arrived this morning...**, and Letter 6.3: **We are happy to confirm...which we ordered two weeks ago....** Compare this with the present perfect which is used when an event in the past relates directly to now, e.g. Letter 6.1: **We have received the trial order...** and Letter 6.4: **The first part of the consignment of wall cupboards has just arrived by rail.**

*Exercise 6.1*

*Complete the following letter from a client to a supplier regarding an order for 30 video-recorders.*

.........: Our ......... No: 3265/32 – 30 video-recorders

Dear Sirs,

We ......... ......... ......... trial .........

......... ......... ......... ......... mentioned

......... which ......... ......... .........

condition. Our van ......... ......... goods

......... ......... ......... ......... yesterday.

We hope ......... ......... ......... .........

position to ......... ......... ......... .........

......... shortly.

In ......... ......... ......... yet to

be .........., we ..........,


*Exercise 6.2*

*Reorder the following to make a letter similar to Letters 6.1 - 6.4:*

```
John Field, Chief Buyer.

as we hope, our customers like the

order larger amounts from

ago (Nos: 7 & 8 of our order). If,

Dear Sir, We are happy to confirm

you. Yours faithfully,

which we ordered two weeks

goods, we shall be pleased to

the arrival of the armchairs
```

*Exercise 6.3*

*Write a letter to Mr B. Trafford of Europac plc at 14 Lewes Road, Dingly, Buckinghamshire MK18 IBH from Mr. R Whitney of Frozen Food Promotions Ltd, 13/25 Goswell Road, Hampstead, London, NW3 6AP. Include the date, references and your order number. Mention:*

- that the first part of the consignment of frozen cooked meals has just arrived.
- that the invoice and the shipment tally perfectly.
- and, as you close, that you are still waiting for the rest of the goods to be delivered.

# Complaints

*Study the model letters, answer the questions and complete the exercises.*

*Letter 7.1*

---

## ALEXANDER
### Ceramic Products
Legrand Dernis (Europe) Group

■■■■■■■■■■■■■■■■■■■■■■■■■■■■■■

176 Miklegate
Sutton
Surrey SMI INF

Tel: 01-785634
Telex: 56438
Fax: 301 876

WIPAK Sales S.A
(London Office)
1 St. James Churchyard
London EC4M 8SH

12 March 19..

Your ref:
Our ref: 143/2A/jl

Dear Sirs,

We have just taken delivery of the articles in our
order No. 143/2A.

We regret to inform you that the bathroom cabinets
(with mirror, strip lighting and **shelf\***, colour: dark
**maritime\* pine\***) are not up to the usual **standard\***.

Could you please make the necessary arrangements for
the **replacement\*** of these articles and their delivery?

In anticipation of a speedy reply, we remain,

Yours faithfully,

*George Kennett*

George Kennett
Manager

a) *Has Mr Kennett dealt with WIPAK Sales before?*
b) *What is his complaint?*
c) *What does he want the company to do?*

*Letter 7.2*

```
Dear Sirs,

We regret to inform you that our consignment of a set
of weight-training equipment was delivered to us in a
very bad state.

You can understand our disappointment.

We are now returning the damaged items and would be
grateful if you would replace them immediately.

Yours faithfully,


John Goddard
```

a) *Is Mr Goddard returning the whole consignment?*
b) *What does he want done?*
c) *How do you know that he is in a hurry?*
d) *What does 'items' refer to?*

*Letter 7.3*

Dear Mr Read,

We acknowledge reception of the **solid\*** pine settees which you sent to us according to our order of the 5th **instant\***.

Although the boxes are **intact\***, when we unpacked them, we discovered that a certain number of the items were broken.

We have told the shipper about the damage and kept the boxes and their contents so that they may be inspected.

Yours faithfully,


Mervyn Little

a) *When did Mr Little find out that some of the items were damaged?*
b) *Who has he reported the problem to?*
c) *Why is he keeping the damaged goods?*
d) *What does 'items' refer to?*

*Letter 7.4*

Dear Sirs,

Your shipment was at last delivered yesterday from the air freight depot.

Unfortunately, I regret to have to inform you that the goods were clearly damaged.

I would therefore be obliged if you would send your representative as soon as possible so that he can **verify\*** the situation himself.

Yours faithfully.


Mark Picard
Managing Director
Eurostat SA

a) *How do you know that Eurostat have been waiting some time for their goods?*
b) *What does 'the situation' refer to in the third paragraph?*

# Drills

1) Although the / boxes / were intact when we unpacked them / we / discovered that a certain number of the / items / were broken.

   a) packets / on arrival / I / digital scales / damaged.
   b) boxes / when we received them / I / infra-red sunray lamps / spoilt.
   c) cases / at the depot / our agent / amchairs / broken.
   d) cardboard boxes / at the office / my assistant / telephone tables / below standard.

2) We / acknowledge reception of the / car alarms / which you sent to us according to our order of the / 5th / instant.

   a) We / cooking ranges / 1st
   b) I / 'Permo Focus' binoculars / 24th
   c) Mr. Wigzell / indoor aerials / 3rd
   d) Our client / 'Shorty' boots with elastic sides / 8th

3) We / regret to inform you that / our consignment of / mobile gas heaters / was delivered to us / today / in a very bad state.

   a) I / shipment / mini-ovens / this morning
   b) The Manager / consignment / spring mattresses / yesterday
   c) I / boxes / pyjamas / 5th August
   d) We / packet / shirts / this afternoon

# Grammar Check

1) **So that** is often used in place of a 'to-infinitive' to express the purpose of doing something. It can be used when the purpose is negative, e.g. **She drove fast so that she wouldn't be late for work**. It can also be used when a person does something to make another person do something else, e.g. **We telephoned New York so that they would know our arrival time**. In Letters 7.3 and 7.4 **so that** is used with the auxiliaries **may** and **can**.

2) In Letter 7.4 **...I regret to have to inform you...** is an example of the use of **have to** expressing a fact rather than the writer's own feelings, i.e. the fact he is obliged to tell them that the goods were damaged.

*Exercise 7.1*

*Complete the following letter from a client to a supplier regarding an order for 10 garden* **sheds**.

```
Dear Sirs,

We ......... ......... delivery of the articles

in our order No. 313/2. Although .........

......... was ......... ......... .........

unpacked it, we regret ......... .........

......... ......... ......... that.........

......... ......... ......... ......... broken.

You can ......... our disappointment.

We ......... ......... ......... .........

......... ......... damage and ......... boxes

......... ......... ......... so that.........

......... ......... ......... .

Yours faithfully,
Jessie Carter, Manageress
```

*Exercise 7.2*

*Reorder the following to make a letter similar to Letters 7.1 - 7.3:*

goods did not come up to their

the freight station in Carlisle. We

regret to inform you that the

the shipper about the damage

at last delivered yesterday at

inspected. Yours faithfullly, Rachel Chan.

contents so that they may be

Dear Sirs, Your shipment was

and kept the boxes and their

usual standard. We have told

*Exercise 7.3 :*

Write a letter from M. Jacques Duhaut, the Managing Director of Billantard SARL, part of the Billac Group, at 78 rue Soriano, B.P. 879 34 F-75634 Paris Cedex 14, to Mr Price-Jones of EUROMAT FOODS at 6 Willicombe Avenue, Croydon CR8 J95, UK. Mention that:

- you have received the canned fish in accordance with your order of the 5th.
- unfortunately, you have to report that the goods are clearly defective.
- you are returning the faulty goods immediately.
- you would like replacements straight away.
- end the letter appropriately.

# Apologies and replies to complaints

*Study the model letters, answer the questions and complete the exercises.*

*Letter 8.1*

---

## SOUVIE LTD  Everything for the home

45 Chapel Road,
Folkestone,
Kent CT20 2EF

Tel: 0303- 76548
Telex: 908675
Fax: 879543

LEVERS CUT GLASS PLC
Cliffe Industrial Estate
Barnsley
Yorks YI9 7TR

10 March 19..
Your ref: LCG/JL
Our ref: GE/km

Order No: 4365 - 30 dozen wine glasses:

Dear Sirs,

In reply to your letter of 3rd March on the subject of the non-delivery of the wine glasses, we have asked our Shipping Department and they inform us that the goods were damaged by the storm we had in this area last week.

You can rest assured[1] that we shall make certain that this order will be **dealt with\*** as soon as possible.

Please accept our apologies for the **inconvenience\***.

Yours faithfully,

George Eastern
Sales Manager

[1] be sure

a) *How did Mr Eastern find out what had happened to the order?*
b) *Why wasn't the order sent off promptly?*
c) *What is he going to do about it?*
d) *What does 'goods' refer to?*

*Letter 8.2*

Dear Miss Colley,

We very much regret that until now we have not been able to send you the computer disk labels you ordered.

We certainly have them in stock, but cannot **locate\*** any invoice in your name. Can you, in order to[1] help us with our **enquiry\***, send us the number and the date of your order?

We assure you[2] that we shall give the matter our **utmost\*** attention immediately we receive your reply.

Yours faithfully,

Peter Derrick

[1] so as to
[2] You can be sure

a) *Why hasn't Mr Derrick been able to send the goods?*
b) *What does he want his client to do?*
c) *How does he show that he values this particular client's custom?*

*Letter 8.3*

Dear Sirs,

We have noticed that we have **overcharged\*** you by £400,
and you will find a **credit note\*** attached for that
amount.

We are in the process of changing computers, which has
led to a certain amount of **duplication\*** of invoices.

As soon as things are back to normal[1], we hope to be
able to continue as usual. Please accept our apologies.

Yours faithfully,


Marita Howard
Clients' Accounts

[1] have returned to normal

*a) Why has Ms Howard sent her client a credit note?*
*b) Why has there been a certain amount of duplication?*

*Letter 8.4*

Dear Madam,

We are very **put out\*** to hear that the wooden spring bed
**frames\*** which we sent you by train became **unfastened\***
during transport and **consequently\*** arrived broken.

We offer our most **profound\*** excuses for this mistake
which was caused by the carelessness of a new packer.

We are ready to accept full **responsibility\*** for the
damage and we have immediately replaced the articles.

Please excuse us for all the inconvenience that this
may have caused you.

Yours faithfully,


Howard Midwinter
Dispatch Dept.

a) *What happened to the articles?*
b) *Whose fault was it?*
c) *What has Mr Midwinter done about the error?*
d) *What does 'articles' refer to?*

# Drills

*Complete the sentences as in the examples. Make changes where necessary :*

1) In reply to your letter of / 3 March on the subject of the non-delivery of the / plastic covered nylon sports bags, / we / have asked our Shipping Department who inform us that the / goods / were **dispatched*** / this morning.

   a) 9 February / circular saws / I / manager / cardboard boxes / sent / yesterday.
   b) 23 June / curtains / we / **foreman*** / packets / shipped / yesterday afternoon.
   c) 5 August / slide projectors / my assistant / Shipping Agent / containers / dispatched / last week.
   d) 8 July / brushed wool jogging suits / we / representative / bales / sent / this morning.

2) We / very much regret that, until now, we have been unable to / send / you / the computer disk labels / that you ordered.

   a) The Sales Manager / send / high-**precision*** astronomical telescopes
   b) We / dispatch / 6/12 V battery chargers
   c) My colleague / ship / 50 tool kits
   d) I / send / car loudspeakers

3) We / were very put out to hear that the / digital calendar watches / which we / sent / by train / were / **crushed*** / during transport.

   a) I / 12V car vacuum cleaners / dispatched / rail / damaged
   b) Mr Laurence / electric paint sprays / shipped / sea / scratched
   c) I / pleated trousers / sent / post / spoilt
   d) We / antique hallstand / dispatched / road / broken

# Grammar Check

1) The past tense and past participle forms of certain irregular verbs are very common in business letters, e.g. **send/sent/sent; let/let/let; take/took/taken; break/broke/broken; get/**

**got/got** (or in the USA often **gotten**); **deal/dealt/dealt; become/ became/become**. Be sure to make a note of them as they occur. In this unit, examples are Letter 8.3 **...which has led to a certain amount of...** and Letter 8.4 **...which we sent you by train became unfastened**.

*Exercise 8.1*

*Complete the following letter from a supplier in answer to a client's complaint about the non-delivery of 10 filing cabinets. Explain that they were damaged by fire in the warehouse last week.*

Dear Sir,

In reply ......... ......... ......... .........

1st April on the subject of ......... .........

......... ......... ......... ......... .........

......... ......... ......... ......... Shipping

Department ......... ......... ......... .........

that ......... ......... ......... .........

......... fire that ......... ......... .........

......... warehouse ......... ......... . As

soon as ......... ......... ......... .........

........., we hope ......... ......... .........

......... ......... ......... usual. Please

......... ......... ......... ......... .........

inconvenience that this may have caused you.

. . . . . . . . .  . . . . . . . . . ,

*Exercise 8.2*

*Rewrite the following to form a letter similar to Letters 8.1 - 8.4*

make sure that this order will be

for all the inconvenience

can rest assured that we shall

dealt with as soon as possible. Please excuse us

faithfully, Oliver Gardner, Export Manager.

send you the settees you ordered. You

that this may have caused you. Yours

that, until now, we have not been able to

Dear Sirs, We very much regret

*Exercise 8.3*

*Write a letter to Mr Ansari, the General Manager of Jishi and Co., PO Box 45, Manama, Bahrain, The Arabian Gulf, from Gerald Arkwright, Sales Manager of Turner Brothers plc of Old Orchard Road, Manchester M7 8LK, UK. Include the date and references and say:*

- that you have received their letter of 9th September.
- that you are sorry for the mistake made in the shipment of their order.
- that the mistake occurred because you are changing computers: this has led to a duplication of orders.
- end appropriately by saying that you are sorry for the inconvenience that the incident may have caused.

# Complaints and replies about payment

Study the model letters, answer the questions and complete the exercises.

*Letter 9.1*

# INTERSERVICE
## Aeronautical Equipment

81, Loughborough Road, Hampden Park Trading Estate
Ditchling, Derbyshire DJ7 KL8  UK
Tel: 087- 4532670 Telex: 143 136

Jacques  Cherrau
ISOTECH  FRANCE
rue  Ampère  -  immeuble  Vomag
89476  PLAISIR  CEDEX
France

Your ref: JC/mt
Our ref: JPF/jd                          1 May 1991


Dear Mr Cherrau,

We would like to draw your attention[1] to our bill of 4
March.

As we have not yet received your payment for the last
two shipments, we would be very grateful if you would
send it as soon as possible.

I am sure that this delay is due[2] to an **oversight\*** in
your accounts department and while awaiting
**settlement\***, I remain,

Yours  faithfully,

A. Littlejohn
Sales  Director

[1] point out
[2] because of, owing to

a)  *What is Mr Littlejohn's main complaint?*
b)  *What does he suggest is the cause of the problem?*

*Letter 9.2*

Dear Sirs,

We wish to remind you that your invoice No. 896/1A
dated 8 August has not yet been settled.

We ask you to give this situation your most **urgent***
attention.

If you have already **transferred*** the amount in
question, please take no notice of this **request***.

We look forward to receiving your next letter.

Yours faithfully,

Ronald Bates
per pro[1]
The Managing Director

[1] on behalf of (also written **pp**)

a)  *What is 'this situation' mentioned in the letter?*
b)  *What could be the purpose of the reply to this letter?*

*Letter 9.3*

Dear Madam,

We have received your letter of 12 September last in which you draw our attention to the fact that we have **overrun\*** the time limit of your last two bills.

As we are experiencing temporary **cash-flow\*** difficulties, we are sending you half of the amount as an **instalment\*** and we shall pay the **remainder\* over\*** the next three months.

We are very grateful for your understanding.

Yours faithfully,

Jeremy Milton

Encl: Cheque

a)  *What was the purpose of the letter written on 12th September?*
b)  *How is the writer trying to overcome the problem?*

*Letter 9.4*

Dear Sirs,

As you are aware[1], our policy has always been to **settle\*** our accounts with the minimum of delay.

However, the damage caused by the **hurricane\*** in the South of England resulted in serious cash-flow problems and we would be very grateful if you would allow us 30 days extra.

Thanking you in advance.

Yours faithfully,


Percival Davey
Accounts Department

[1] As you know

a) *What does 'as you are aware' suggest?*
b) *Why has the company had to spend a great deal of money lately?*

# Drills

*Complete the sentences as in the examples. Make changes where necessary:*

1) We / would like to draw your attention to our / bill / of 4 March.

   a) I / statement of account / 8 August.
   b) The manager / cheque / 20 January
   c) We / receipt / 4 March.
   d) I / advertisement / 18 October.

2) The damage / caused by the hurricane / resulted in serious cash-flow problems and / we / would be very grateful if you would allow us / 30 / days extra.

   a) the damage / the rain / delays / I / a **fortnight***
   b) the delay / the **strike*** / shortages / the staff / a week
   c) the **hold-up*** / cold weather / problems / the manager / a month
   d) the **stoppage*** / the flood / hold-ups / we / a few days

3) We / wish to remind you that your invoice No. / 896-1A / dated / 8 August / has not yet been settled.

   a) I / account / A-23-13 / 9 January
   b) The manager / bills / 325-X32-1 & 2 / 11 February
   c) Our Accounts Department / account / B43-430-1 / 23 March
   d) Mr Springfield / bills / X432-76 & 7 / 14 December

# Grammar Check

1) When a verb consists of two or more words, we usually put the adverb in the mid-position after the first part of the verb. Note the following examples - Letter 9.1: **...we have not *yet* received....** Letter 9.2: **has not *yet* been settled..; If you have *already* transferred....** Letter 9.4: **..our policy has *always* been....**

2) In business letters **as** is often used to mean **because**, e.g. in Letter 9.1: **As we have not yet received your payment...** and Letter 9.3: **As we are experiencing temporary cash-flow difficulties....**

3) In Letter 9.2 **We wish to remind you...** is a more formal way of stating **We would like to remind you....**

*Exercise 9.1*

*Complete the following letter from a supplier complaining to a client about the non-payment of his last consignment of goods.*

Dear Sirs,

We ........ ........ ........ ........ ........

........ ........ ........ ........ ........

12th February. As ........ ........ ........

........ ........ ........ settlement ........

........ February, we would like ........

........ ........ ........ ........ utmost

attention. If you ........ ........ ........

........ ........ ........ in question,

please take ........ ........ ........ ........

request. I am ........ ........ ........

........ ........ due to an oversight in your

```
accounts department and while ........ ........ ,

we remain,

Yours faithfully,

George Hicks, Accounts Department
```

*Exercise 9.2*

*Rewrite the following to form a letter similar to Letters 9.1 - 9.4:*

```
settled and we would appreciate it if you would send
```

```
very grateful for your
```

```
Yours faithfully, Eric Jones, Customer Accounts.
```

```
that your invoice No 896/1A dated 8th
```

```
understanding in this matter.
```

```
August has not yet been
```

```
payment as soon as possible. We are
```

```
Dear Sir, We wish to remind you
```

*Exercise 9.3*

*Write a letter from Mr J. Bressler of MOD INSTRUMENTATION at 8 Lovell Street, Howell Trading Estate, Redhill, Surrey SU7 TW3 (Tel: 076-98657, Telex: 876 343) to Mr O. Linqvist, 12 Rödenhalser Gaten, 98672 Stockholm, Sweden. Include references and state that:*

- you have certainly received their letter of 8 January regarding the non-settlement of your order A/8675.
- you have temporary cash-flow problems.
- you are sending him half of the amount due.
- you will pay the remainder over the next three months.
- thank him in advance and end appropriately.

# Status enquiries

*Study the model letters, answer the questions and complete the exercises.*

*Letter 10.1*

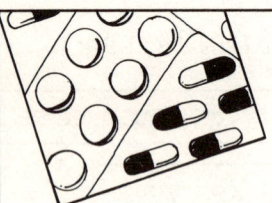

# PHILIPE
# *Pharmaceuticals*

8 Bishopsgate, Charminster
Bournmouth, Dorset BH8 8PY
Tel: 0202/372321 Telex: 43208
Fax: 0202/87654

The Manager
Barclays Bank AG
Ueberseering 5
1000 Berlin 10
Germany
5 March 19.

*Your ref:*
*Our ref:* BB/D

Dear Sirs,

We have just received an important order from the
company whose name you will find enclosed.

Could you please let us have full information on this
company's financial position.

We would particularly like to know if the company
enjoys a **sound\*** financial situation and if we can let
them have goods up to a credit limit of DM 50 000.

You can rest assured that this information will be kept
strictly **confidential\***.

Yours faithfully,

Donald Spencer
General Manager

a) *Why is Mr Spencer asking the bank for information?*
b) *What has Mr Spencer done to protect the confidentiality of his client?*
c) *What does he particularly want to know?*

*Letter 10.2*

Dear Sirs,

We would be very grateful if we could obtain information about Carlton Incorporated, Seattle, Washington, USA, who would like to open an account and who have given us your name as a reference.

We know that you often have business dealings with them, so[1] we thought that you, better than anyone else, could give us information about their financial situation. Do you think that we could safely do business with them on a credit basis?

In the hope of a speedy reply, we enclose an international reply coupon.

Yours faithfully,

Milton Jackson
Export Manager

[1] therefore

a) *What is the connection between Carlton Incorporated and Milton Jackson's company?*
b) *What does he particularly want to know?*
c) *What has he done to ensure a quick reply?*

*Letter 10.3*

Dear Sirs,

We would like to know your opinion on the subject of
the Wadja company in Budapest, who have given your name
as a reference.

Before finally **committing*** ourselves, we would be
obliged if you would give us your opinion on the
quality of their work and of their after sales service.

We assure you that all information that you give us
will be treated confidentially.

Yours faithfully,

Irene St John
Manageress

a) *What does Ms St John want to know before she does business with the Wadja company?*

*Letter 10.4*

Dear Sirs,

Baker Jackson plc have contacted us with a view to[1]
placing an important order for household goods.

They have given us your name and address and we would
therefore be very grateful if you would supply us with
information on their financial situation as soon as
possible.

Although we are sure of their ability to pay, we would
like confirmation that their financial situation
guarantees **quarterly*** payments of up to $50 000.

Needless to say,[2] all information will remain
confidential.

Yours faithfully,

Jack Funnel
Sales Director

[1]  with the intention of
[2]  it is not necessary to say, it goes without saying

*a)  What sort of order has Baker Jackson placed?*
*b)  How often will they be required to pay?*

# Drills

*Complete the sentences as in the examples. Make changes where necessary:*

1)  We / have just received an important order from the / company / whose name you will find on the enclosed slip.

    a)  The Director / business / we spoke about.
    b)  I / corporation / you mentioned.
    c)  We / organization / I mentioned on the 'phone yesterday.
    d)  My partner / agency / he mentioned last week.

2)  We / would particularly like to know if this / company / enjoys a sound financial situation and if we can let them have goods up to a credit limit of / DM 50 000.

    a)  I / business / machinery / 100,000 FF.
    b)  Mr Laurence / organization / merchandise / $50,000.
    c)  We / store / soft furnishings / 2,000,000 pesetas.
    d)  We / company / machine tools / £50,000.

3)  Before finally committing / ourselves, / we would be obliged if you would give / us / your opinion on the quality of their work and of their after sales service.

    a)  myself / I / financial standing.
    b)  herself / Mrs Jackson / ability to deliver on time.
    c)  themselves / the partners / ability to fulfil orders quickly.
    d)  ourselves / we / sales network.

# Grammar Check

1)  Letter 10.1: **Whose** in relative clauses is generally used to refer to people, e.g. **That's the man whose lorry turned over.** It is always followed by a noun.

2)  In this unit note the word order in indirect questions, e.g. Letter 10.1: **We would particularly like to know if this company enjoys.... Whether** can be used in place of **if** in this kind of sentence which should not be confused with a

conditional clause. Note the word-order differences in:

Letter 10.1: **Does the company enjoy...?**
**We would particularly like to know if the company enjoys...**
(No question mark because it is not a question.)

Letter 10.2: **Could we obtain information about...?**
**We would be very grateful if we could obtain information about...**
(No question mark because it is not a question.)

Letter 10.2: **Could we safely do business with them?**
**Do you think that we could safely do business with them?**
(A question mark because it is still a question.)

*Exercise 10.1*

*Complete the following letter to a bank asking for confidential information about a potential client.*

Dear Sir,

We ......... ......... ......... .........

......... ......... from the company whose

......... ......... ......... ......... .........

......... ......... slip. Could you .........

......... ......... ......... .........

information ......... ......... .........

......... position. We know that .........

......... have ......... ......... .........

......... so ......... ......... that ........,

......... ......... ......... else, could ........

......... ......... ......... ......... ........

situation. ......... ......... think that........

......... ......... ......... ......... .........

them? Needless to say ........ information

......... ......... ......... .

........ faithfully,

Charles Macintosh, Manager

*Exercise 10.2*

*Rewrite the following to form a letter similar to Letters 10.1 - 10.4:*

sound financial situation and if we can

would like to open an account and

reply coupon. Yours faithfully, Karl Rauch.

of Seattle, Washington, USA, who

limit of DM 50,000. In the hope of

could obtain information about Calton Incorporated

let them have goods up to a credit

like to know if this company enjoys a

as a reference. We would particularly

a speedy reply, we enclose an international

who have given us your name

Dear Sir, We would be very grateful if we

*Exercise 10.3*

*Write a letter from one of the companies in a previous unit to the Manager of the Banque Nationale de Paris, 56 rue Nationale, 74500 Evian-les-Bains, France, asking for their opinion of Bayart Père Fils & Cie. Mention that:*

— they gave the bank's name as a reference.
— although you are sure of their ability to pay their bills, you would like to know if they would be able to meet quarterly bills of up to 6 000 000 FF.
— the bank can be sure that the information will be treated as confidential.
— end appropriately.

# Cancellations and alterations

*Study the model letters, answer the questions and complete the exercises.*

*Letter 11.1*

# PROPEC PLASTICS PLC

Späthstraße 43/45
3240 Helmstedt
Germany

Tel: 05051/8706-75
Telex: 72 7864

INSTRONEX INTERNATIONAL
12-5-35 Mishiyama-dai
Sakiachi-cho
Hiroshima-Fu 365
Japan

Your ref: A/147B
Our ref:II/JZ

Dear Sir,

We are obliged to inform you that a mistake has
**slipped\*** into our order No. A/147B of 5 October last.
Instead of:

Storage case for 18 compact disks,

it should read:

Storage box for 10 audio cassettes.

Please excuse us for this **regrettable\* incident\***.

Yours faithfully,

*Jürgen Zimmerman*

Jürgen Zimmerman
Shipping Department

a) *How does Mr Zimmerman excuse himself for the error?*
b) *What is the error exactly?*

*Letter 11.2*

Dear Sirs,

On 4 January we ordered a graphic equalizer VOXIMOND which should be delivered at the end of the month.

We have, however, **discovered*** that our present stock is **sufficient*** for the coming month and we would like to cancel the order.

I hope that, in view of[1] our **long-standing*** dealings with you, you will accept this change.

Yours faithfully,


George Remington
Manager

---

[1] because of


a) *About how long has Mr Remington been waiting for this order?*
b) *What does it seem has happened during this time?*

*Letter 11.3*

Dear Sirs,

We are sorry to learn from your letter of 9 October
that it is impossible for you to **fulfil\*** our order No.
875-326 according to the **stipulated\*** details.

We have to remind you that we **insisted\*** the delivery
date should be **adhered\*** to and now see ourselves
obliged to cancel the order.

Yours faithfully,


William Ferry
Sales Manager

*a) What did the letter of 9 October tell Mr Ferry?*
*b) Why has Mr Ferry cancelled the order?*

*Letter 11.4*

Dear Madam,

Re: Our order No:A/5423 for half-socks

As you have not got these articles in stock, we would
be obliged if you would cancel our order of batches of
8 pairs of half-socks and replace it with batches of 10
pairs of half-stockings (colour the same as the half-
socks). Please find enclosed a **revised\*** order form.

We should be obliged if you would confirm as soon as
possible that this change is acceptable.

We hope to receive a **favourable\*** reply,

Yours faithfully,


Claire Conroy
Chief Buyer

Enc.

*a) Why is Ms Conroy cancelling the original order?*
*b) What is enclosed in the letter?*

## Drills

*Complete the sentences as in the examples. Make changes where necessary:*

1) We / are obliged to inform you that a mistake has slipped into / our / order No: / A-147B of / 5th October last.
   Instead of: / Maroon pleated trousers
   it should read: / Grey pleated trousers

   a) I / B-4325 / 8th January / Jackets 100% cotton / Jackets 100% brushed cotton.
   b) Our customer / A-34/23-1 / 12th October / stereo headphones / mini-stereo headphones.
   c) Our customers / X-435 / 15th March / 'Charlotte' dolls / 'Laurie' dolls.
   d) We / 4532-1 / 17th February / Batch of 10 video cassettes 2 x 120 mn Ref: 132.12 / Batch of 12 video cassettes 2 x 140 mn Ref: 132.10.

2) On / 4th January / we / ordered a cleaning kit for a VHS video recorder / which should be delivered / at the end of the month.

   a) 9th July / my assistant / 5 shower curtains 80 x 150 cm. / this week.
   b) 8th August / I / 10 leather office armchairs / at the end of the week.
   c) 18th June / our customers / 100 Grandfather, cotton nightshirts / today.
   d) 10th November / we / 20 pocket electronic chess games / in a few days.

3) As / you / have not got these articles in stock, / we / would be obliged if you would cancel our order for / 6 HONDA 750 motorcycles / and replace them with 6 (rough terrain) YAMAHAS

   a) your shop / I / 10 GEC portable black-and-white TV sets / 10 GEC portable colour TV sets.
   b) they / the manageress / 6 electric toasters / 6 electric mini ovens.
   c) the warehouse / our clients / 25 articulated desk-top lamps, black / 10 black and 15 red.
   d) you / we / "après-ski" boots in three colours / blue après-ski boots with laces.

# Grammar Check

1) In this unit note the two meanings of **obliged: We are obliged to inform you ...** (Letter 11.1) and **We now see ourselves obliged to cancel ...** (Letter 11.3). Here the meaning is **must** or **have to**. On the other hand in Letter 4.4. **We would be obliged if...** means "We would be grateful if..."

2) **Have to** and **must** are often interchangeable. However, with **have to** the writer is not expressing his own feelings, but only the facts, e.g **We have to remind you...** (Letter 11.3). In this sense **have to** has the same meaning as **to be obliged to** in the examples above.

3) Note that American usage for **As you have not got...** in Letter 11.4 is **As you do not have...**

### Exercise 11.1

*Complete the following letter cancelling an order because the supplier does not have the goods in stock.*

Dear Madam,

As ......... ......... ......... .........

......... ......... ......... stock, we would be

......... ......... ......... ......... .........

......... ......... No. 73891/43A. I hope that,

in view ......... ......... ......... .........

......... ......... you, you ......... .........

......... change. We look to receiving .........

```
........ reply,

........ ........ ,
```

Margaret Heath, Manageress

*Exercise 11.2*

*Rewrite the following to form a letter similar to Letters 11.1 - 11.4:*

of double sided, double density 3½"

order form.  Yours faithfully, Max

stock, we would be obliged if

cases of DS, DD 5¼" floppy

our order No. 875-326 according

that it is impossible for you to fulfil

you would cancel our order of 6 cases

to the stipulated details.  As

Kaminsky, Overseas Sales.

from your letter of 9th October

disks.  Please find enclosed a revised

Dear Sir, We are sorry to learn

micro floppy disks and replace it with 6

you have not got these articles in

*Exercise 11.3*

*Write a letter (adding references, date etc) from Gerald Booth of Intertech, 8 Old Orchard Road, Upper Beeding, Surrey SR8 UK6, to Franco Hermanos of Simex Electro S.A., Pau Claris, 169 - 20 39004 Santander, Spain apologizing that:*

- there was an error in your last order.
- instead 200 F/6736A transistors, the order should have read 200 F6836B transistors.
- you would be grateful if he would let you know if they can change the order.

*Study the model letters, answer the questions and complete exercises.*

*Letter 12.1*

---

# BURNLEY PLASTICS

Burnley House, Coronation Road, Bicester, Oxfordshire OX6 0XD.
Tel: (865) 3455643   Telex: 856 345 G

Montri Chilananda
UNICUM TECHNOLOGY
12 Bukit Timar Road
Bangkok
Thailand

19 January 19..

**Your ref:**
**Our ref:** MC/jp

Dear Mr Chilananda,

We have pleasure in announcing the visit of our new representative, Brian Rothwell, to Bangkok with a complete set of our new samples. He will call on you the course of next week[1].

I am sure that you will find Mr Rothwell both pleasant and obliging[2], and that you will appreciate his **professional\*** qualities.

I hope that you will offer him a warm welcome in Bangkok and place some orders, which will receive our utmost attention.

Yours sincerely,

*John Philips.*

John Philips
Managing Director

¹ some time next week
² helpful

*a) Who is Brian Rothwell?*
*b) What is he taking with him to Bangkok?*

*Letter 12.2*

---

Dear Mr Sutherland,

We learn with great pleasure that you are interested in
our type of merchandise. We are happy to inform you
that our representative, Duncan Shoesmith, will very
shortly be in your area with a complete **assortment***  of
our latest products as well as our current range.

We would be grateful if you would let us know as soon
as possible whether a visit is **convenient*** so that we
can arrange a meeting.

Yours faithfully,

Harry Moss
Sales Manager

---

*a) What prompted Harry Moss to write to this company?*
*b) What is the purpose of the letter?*

*Letter 12.3*

---

Dear Sir,

Our new representative in your area, Bill Davey, will
call to see you in the course of the coming week.

He will inform you himself of the date and time of his
visit and we hope that you will offer him a warm
welcome. If you wish to place an order, you can be sure
that it will be treated with our usual care and
attention.

We hope that this arrangement is acceptable to you.

Yours faithfully,

Nicky Marchant
Overseas Sales Manager

---

a) When is Bill Davey going to make his visit?
b) How will the client know when he is coming?

Letter 12.4

Dear Madam,

We are very happy to introduce John Higgins, our new
area representative.

He will show you, on our behalf[1] a collection of our
latest models. We would particularly like to draw your
attention to[2] the exceptional quality of the models in
Nylon which sell at extremely **competitive\*** prices.

We hope that you will **favour\*** us with an order which,
it goes without saying[3], will be processed with the
utmost care.

Yours faithfully,


Martin Goldsmith
Manager


[1] for us

[2] show you

[3] needless to say / it is not necessary to say


a) Who is John Higgins?
b) What kind of product is Martin Goldsmith trying to promote?


# Drills

Complete the sentences as in the examples. Make changes where
necessary:

1) Our / new representative / in your area, / Bill Davey, / will
   call to see you / in the course of the coming week.

   a) My / commercial traveller / John Harrington / shortly.
   b) Our / representative / Marie Russell / soon.
   c) My / colleagues / Philip Roberts and Oscar Peters / at the
      beginning of next week.

2) We / have pleasure in announcing the visit of / our / new / representative, Duncan Shoesmith, / to / Bangkok / with a complete set of our new samples. /He will call on you / in the course of next week.

   a) I / representative / Madeleine Godart / Paris / samples of our new range / in a few days' time.
   b) Mr Jackson / assistant / Peter Philips / Cologne / our brochures / shortly.
   c) We / colleague / Edward Anderson / Vienna / our latest products / at the beginning of the week.

3) We / are happy to inform you that our / representative, / Colin Blackwell, / will / very shortly / be in your area with a complete assortment of our / latest products / as well as / our current range.

   a) I / commercial traveller / Charles Sarvan / during the week / padded jackets / multi-coloured jogging suits.
   b) Mrs Saville / assistant / Isabel Pierce / soon / multi-purpose cardboard filing boxes / pull-out plastic filing systems.
   c) We / partner / Michael Clarke / next week / range of non-stick kitchenware / cutlery.

## Grammar Check

In this Unit, note the various ways prepositions are used:
     prep + **ing** - Letter 12.1 - **in announcing** (see also Unit 2)
     verb + prep - Letter 12.1 - **call on**
                            Letter 12.4 - **sell at**
     noun + prep -  Letter 12.1 - **a set of, the course of**
                            Letter 12.2 - **an assortment of**
                            Letter 12.4 - **a collection of, the quality of**
     prep + noun -  Letter 12.4 - **in Nylon**
     verb + (pro)noun + prep - Letter 12.3 - **inform you of**
                                        Letter 12.4 - **draw your attention to**
     adjective + prep - Letter 12.2 - **interested in**

*Exercise 12.1*

*Complete the following letter introducing a new representative:*

Dear Madam,

We learn with ........ ......... ..........

.......... .......... .......... .......... ..........

.......... .......... merchandise.

We are happy ......... .......... .........

.......... .......... .........., Mark Blackwell,

will very shortly be ......... .......... .........

.......... .......... ......... assortment .........

.......... ..........products as ......... .........

.......... .......... range. I ......... .........

......... find Mr Blackwell both .........

.......... .........., and that ......... .........

.......... .......... .......... qualities.

.......... ..........,

Greg Thomson

*Exercise 12.2*

*Reorder the following to make a letter similar to Letters 12.1 - 12.4.*

visit is convenient so that

of our new samples. He will call on

hope that this arrangement suits you. Yours

our new representative, Hussain Dhaif, to

we can arrange a meeting. We

soon as possible whether a | in announcing the visit of

you in the course of next week. We would be grateful

Dear Sirs, We have pleasure

faithfully, Carl Linderman.

if you would let us know as

Bahrain with a complete set

*Exercise 12.3*

*Write a letter (include the date and references) from Hans Hassler the Director of Nelco Distribution 3, place de la Gare, B.P. 56, 91436 Lausanne, Switzerland to Mr Lily of Raleigh Precision Tools, 8 South Street, Haverhill, Suffolk CB9 9QL, UK, introducing a new representative, Michel Gaillard. Inform Mr Lily that*

- Mr Gaillard will come and see him in the course of the following week.
- he will present a collection of the latest models.
- the stainless steel goods are of an exceptionally high quality and sell at a very competitive price.
- you hope that he will give Mr Gaillard a warm welcome as well as some orders, which you will of course process with the utmost care.

# PART TWO
## SUBJECTS FOR FURTHER PRACTICE

# Insurance

*Study the model letters, answer the questions and complete the exercises.*

*Letter 13.1*
*Thanking a client for a completed proposal form and enclosing a cover note.*

---

Dear Mr Jones,

We thank you for your letter of 12 July which was attached to the **proposal form\***.

We are writing to inform you that our staff are now preparing your insurance policy which you will receive between now and the end of the month. In the meantime[1] you are, of course, covered[2].

Please find the **cover note\*** enclosed.

Yours faithfully,


Jeremy Baines
Chief **Underwriter.\***

---

[1] meanwhile
[2] protected


a) *The letter written on 12 July had **Encl:** at the bottom. Why?*
b) *Why did Mr Baines send the cover note and not the policy?*

*Letter 13.2*
## Asking for **compensation*** from a supplier for goods damaged

Dear Sirs,

We regret to inform you that some of the goods sent by
our Agent in St. Malo on the cargo ship <u>Lincoln</u> arrived
in a very bad state. Please find enclosed a report from
the Customs Officials.

You will notice that they **estimate*** the damage to be
£500.

The cargo was fully insured against all risks by our
Hull office. We request you to accept the damage as
**evaluated*** by your own expert and settle the **claim*** at
an early date.

Yours faithfully,


George Page

Encl:


a)  *What does Mr Page want the supplier to do?*
b)  *What is the* **Encl:** *in this letter?*

*Letter 13.3*
## *Requesting indemnity from a shipper for damaged goods.*

Dear Sirs,
When your containers arrived in Hamburg by lorry this
morning, the shipping agents noticed that several of
the boxes in your consignment had been damaged.

On being notified about the goods, we immediately
ordered our **assessor** to examine the cargo. The articles
are complete but some of them have been spoilt, for
example:

- 2 antique walnut tables.
- 12 sets of Chippendale chairs.

Please find attached the assessor's report in
triplicate as well as a letter from the shipping agent
confirming that the damage was noticed immediately the
lorry arrived at the depot.

We would appreciate it if you would get in touch with
the insurers about the problem. The insurance
certificate number is P/96106.

In the interim[1], we would be grateful if you would
replace the damaged goods mentioned above as we have
customers awaiting delivery.

Yours faithfully,


J. Laurence


Encl: 2

Copy to: Shipping Agent

[1] meanwhile

a) *What are the enclosures in this case?*
b) *What does the client want the shipper to do?*

*Exercise 13*

Write a letter to a supplier complaining that Flight DA 765 arrived in Gatwick Airport this morning as expected, but when:

- your agent inspected the cargo he noticed that one of the boxes in container No.12 had been damaged.
- you contacted your insurance representative in Brighton (who agreed to be present when the box was opened).
- he found several of the articles were spoilt.
- you are sending his report.
- you would like the supplier to make a claim with the underwriters.
- Mention that, because of this mishap, you are in a very **embarrassing*** situation as regards your customers.
- Ask the supplier to send you replacements by air freight, as soon as possible.

# Appointing agents

*Study the model letters, answer the questions and complete the exercises.*

*Letter 14.1*
*Offering an agency*

---

Dear Sirs,

We have been selling a **considerable\*** quantity of
English **preserves\*** to different parts of France and are
interested in **appointing\*** an agent to **explore\*** the
market and develop the trade further.

The products in question are a wide selection of jams
and honey. Your name was suggested as agent by Pommet
Frères of Dijon, and on their **recommendation\***, we would
like to offer you the **sole\*** agency for France.

Goods will be consigned to you according to your
instructions since¹ we are only familiar with the
tastes and particular requirements of customers in the
north-east and **realize\*** that these must **vary\*** from
region to region. We are enclosing our price list which
will give you some idea of the **varieties\*** we produce.

Since we realize the difficulties of introducing a new
product to local buyers, we are willing to pay a
commission of 15% on **net\*** sales. We are sure that this
relationship will be **mutually\*** **profitable\*** and hope
that you will accept our offer.

We would very much appreciate an early reply, so that
we can prepare our introductory offers in good time.

Yours faithfully,


Jason Whitney

---

¹ as, because, as it is true that

a) *How do you think this company sold its products before they decided to appoint an agent?*
b) *How does Mr Whitney try to make his offer attractive?*

*Letter 14.2*
*Accepting the offer of an agency*

Dear Mr Wilson,

Thank you for your letter of 7 February offering us an agency for your potted meats. We would be glad to accept the offer. We must point out, however, that only a sole agency would be worthwhile as the **scope*** for your potted meats here is somewhat limited because of local competition; besides, the preference for fresh foods here would also make it difficult to extend the market for English potted meats rapidly. In these circumstances, we feel that competition from another agent would not make our efforts worthwhile.

If you give us your sole agency for France, we feel sure that our wide marketing experience and valuable contacts will enable us to introduce your goods successfully in this country.

Yours sincerely,

Henri Biquet

a) *What reason does Mr Biquet give for wanting the sole agency?*
b) *What is one of the problems when trying to sell English foodstuffs in France?*

*Exercise 14*

*You are a UK firm interested in becoming the agent of a French manufacturer of agricultural products. Write a letter which includes the following points:*

- you were very much impressed by the quality of their agricultural products which you recently saw in action in France.
- you have seen their latest catalogue, and you are interested to know if they have considered appointing an agent in the UK.
- point out that you are a leading firm of importers and distributors of many years' standing.
- you have an extensive sales organization and a very wide knowledge of the UK market.
- you feel that their products would sell very well.
- you are prepared to enter into a business relationship with them.
- you are also interested in handling a sole agency which you feel would be to your mutual advantage.
- you would like to know if they are interested in these proposals.

# Overseas payments

*Study the model letters, answer the questions and complete the exercises.*

*Letter 15.1*
*Replying to a large order requesting to pay by credit*

---

Dear Ms Sanderson,

Thank you for your enquiry regarding our range of fire-fighting equipment.

We supply such equipment **throughout\*** the world for use by companies such as yourselves, and will be glad to provide a large order against a letter of **credit\*** issued through a **reputable\*** international bank.

We look forward, therefore, to receiving a letter of credit in due course[1], when your order will be **processed\*** in the usual way.

Yours sincerely,


Phillip Lemington,
Managing Director

---

[1] at the proper time


a) *How does Mr Lemington want the client to pay for his order?*
b) *When will they process the order?*

## Letter 15.2
### Confirming an order against a letter of credit

Dear Sirs,

Re: Your Order No. JK/9630.

We acknowledge with thanks the receipt of the above order. We are in the process of[1] preparing the magnetic white display boards for shipment.

Our agent has informed us that you will arrange payment by Letter of Credit in our favour[2], valid until 30th June, 19—. These terms are acceptable to us.

As soon as the credit has been confirmed by our bank, the goods will be shipped as instructed.

Yours faithfully,


John Wheeler,
Sales Manager

[1] currently occupied with
[2] to our advantage, for us


a) How does Mr Wheeler know that a letter of credit will be arranged?
b) When will the goods be shipped?

## Letter 15.3
### *Advising that a letter of credit has been opened*

```
Dear Sirs,

With reference to your letter of 19 March, we write to
inform you that we have instructed the Banque Nationale
de Paris in Lyon to open a credit for £5000 in your
favour, valid until 30 June, 1995.

This credit will be confirmed by Barclays Bank in
Guernsey and will be issued* when your draft* is
received at this bank.

Please make sure that all necessary documents are
attached: Bill of Lading* in duplicate, 1 Customs
Invoice, Insurance cover for £7500, 4 separate
Commercial Invoices.

Yours faithfully,

Peter Harrington,
Chief Accountant
```

a) To which bank will the customer be sending his payment?
b) What will he send with the documents?


### *Exercise 15*

*Write a letter to a company informing them that:*

- you acknowledge reception of their order sent on 1 May.
- your representative, Mr Blunt, has informed you that the goods are ready for shipment.
- you note that they will pay by means of a irrevocable letter of credit valid until 1 March.
- when you have been informed that the credit has been opened, the goods will be packed and sent according to their instructions.

# Job applications

*Study the model letters, answer the questions and complete the exercises.*

*Letter 16.1*
*Applying for a job (1)*

---

Dear Sirs,

I wish to apply for the post of **bilingual\*** secretary at AGCOM Ltd, as advertised in <u>The Times</u> on Monday 5 October, 1988.

The attached **CV\*** gives details of my career and qualifications up to this moment, which in outline are as follows:

Since **gaining\*** a BA in 1982, I have successfully completed part-time courses in French and German.

For the past 6 years I have been a private secretary in the Overseas Sales department at Selby Ltd, with particular responsibility for all overseas correspondence. During this time I have successfully introduced a completely new **filing system\*** and modernized the whole office routine.

Having worked at this level for some time, I now wish to seek further responsibility in this **field\*** and would like to take up the **challenge\*** of a new position. I would be grateful, therefore, if you would allow me the **opportunity\*** of meeting with you and your colleagues to discuss my **suitability\***.


Yours faithfully,
Kathleen O'Houlihan

---

a) *Why is Ms O'Houlihan sending her CV to this company?*
b) *What new things has she started in her present office?*

*Letter 16.2*
*Applying for a job (2)*

For the attention of Mr Trulle

Dear Mr Trulle,

Having worked for the past four years as the only
secretary in a **thriving\*** small business, I would like
to apply for the post of **executive\*** secretary as
advertised in <u>The Guardian</u> on Tuesday, 12 January 19—.

As private secretary to the owner of James Young plc in
Southampton, I was not only **responsible\*** for the day to
day running of the office, but for all overseas
correspondence, mostly in Spanish and Portuguese as we
exported to many South American countries. I was also
responsible for the more personal work of making
private **appointments\***, **vetting\*** telephone calls and
visitors and organizing Mr Young's paperwork and
correspondence.

With the above experience behind me, I am **thoroughly\***
familiar with the duties of an executive secretary and
believe that I will certainly come up to all your
**expectations\***.

I enclose my CV and would be grateful if you would give
me the **opportunity\*** to discuss my qualifications with
you in person. I would be happy to attend an interview
at your convenience, and can be reached on my
answerphone at 01-671 986.

Yours sincerely,
Jeremy Hinchcliffe

a) *What was Mr Hinchcliffe's previous position?*
b) *What does he ask Mr Trulle to do?*

*Letter 16.3*
*Applying for a job (3)*

Post of Tourist Information Assistant.

Dear Sirs,

With reference to your advertisement in today's <u>Le Monde</u>, I would like apply for the above post. Details of my qualifications and experience are as follows:

I am a **graduate\*** from the University of Kent with a B.A. degree in Modern Languages (French and Spanish). I also have the Diplôme Superieur in Business French from the Alliance Française in London.

After graduating in 1987, I worked for an advertising agency as a **proof-reader\*** for their monthly magazine dealing with French **wholesale\*** trade. During this time, I attended evening classes in **supervisory\*** management and data processing.

I am sure that, given the **opportunity\***, I will be able to do justice to all aspects of the work entrusted to me as a Tourist Information Assistant. My spoken French is **fluent\*** and I am **thoroughly\*** familiar with many areas of France having studied in Grenoble for a year and made many **excursions\*** from there.

I hope that you will consider my application **sympathetically\***.

Yours faithfully,

Rita Faulkner

a) *What did Ms Faulkner do after she graduated?*
b) *How did she acquire her command of French?*

*Exercise 16*

*Write a letter to a company advertising in* <u>The Guardian</u> *for a shorthand typist.*

- mention where you saw the advertisement and ask them to consider you for the post.
- tell them how long you have been employed as an audio-typist, giving details of your typing and shorthand speeds.
- say that you have recently updated your qualifications by taking a course in computer studies. Mention your competence in Wordstar 5.5 and D.Base 3.
- tell them how old you are and that you have a clean driving licence.
- enclose your CV and copies of three **testimonials***.
- end by saying that you hope they will give the opportunity of an interview.

# Replies to job applications

*Study the model letters, answer the questions and complete the exercises.*

*Letter 17.1*
*Calling an applicant for interview*

---

Dear Miss Billings,

Thank you for your letter applying for the position of
secretary.

I shall be grateful if you could come here for an
interview on Wednesday next, 13 March, at 2.30p.m.

If that day or time is not convenient for you, I would
appreciate it if you could let my secretary know, and I
will try to arrange the interview for a date and time
that is suitable for both of us.

Yours sincerely,

Peter Dodgson,
Personnel Manager

---

a) *When does Mr Dodgson want Miss Billings to come for an
   interview?*
b) *What does he want her to do if she cannot come on Wednesday 13
   March?*

## Letter 17.2
### Confirmation of employment

```
Dear Mr Jackson,

With reference to your letter of Monday 12 January, I
am pleased to confirm the offer of a position as
systems analyst in this company.

Enclosed are three copies of our contract of
employment. Please sign two of these and return them to
my secretary as soon as possible. We have also enclosed
a leaflet giving you full details of our pension fund*,
our luncheon voucher* scheme, the sports club and the
annual outing*.

If you have any queries about the terms of the contract
itself, please do not hesitate* to contact me.

Yours sincerely,

Rosemary Giggins,
Director
```

a) *What does Ms Giggins want Mr Jackson to do?*
b) *Why would Mr Jackson contact Ms Giggins again?*

### Letter 17.3
### *Turning down an applicant after interview*

Dear Mr Fish,

Thank you for your recent visit regarding employment.

After considerable **deliberation*** in the light[1] of our conversation last week, I have come to the conclusion that we cannot at present offer you employment at our offices.

As I mentioned when we met, I will keep your application on file for future reference as we regularly look for extra or **replacement*** staff.

I am glad you came and explained your **capabilities*** so well, and hope that you do not find this decision too disappointing.

Yours sincerely,


Donald Hobson,
Recruitment

---

[1] considering, taking into account

a) *How long did Mr Hobson take to come to a decision about Mr Fish?*
b) *How does he try to lessen Mr Fish's disappointment?*

### *Exercise 17*

*Write a letter from Mr Pattison, of Recruitment, to a candidate, Miss Foxwell, for the post of bilingual secretary;*

— thank her for applying for the post.
— say that you would like to take her application a stage further and that you would like her to come for an interview.
— mention the date and the time.
— ask her to let you know if that day or time is not suitable. You will then try to arrange the interview at a day and time more convenient to her.
— end by saying that you look forward to meeting her in person.

# Personal References

Study the model letters, answer the questions and complete the exercises.

*Letter 18.1*
*Asking permission to give a person's name as a referee*

```
Dear Mr Aubert,

I am about to apply for the position of Sales
Representative at Jack Rothwell & Co. in Madrid. I
would very much appreciate it if I could include your
name in my list of references.

As you are familiar with my work at Llama Gabilondo y
Cia, S.A., you will be able to give Jack Rothwell a
fair evaluation of my capabilities.

I enclose a stamped, addressed envelope for your reply.

Yours sincerely,

John Bridges
```

a) *What post is Mr Bridges applying for?*
b) *Why does he think that Mr Aubert can give him a good reference?*

*Letter 18.2*
## *Asking a referee to send a reference directly to a potential employer*

Dear Mr Gordon,

I am applying for the position of bilingual secretary with Trans-World Travel in Heidelberg.

As you gave me every **encouragement\*** to continue with my study of German and helped me prepare for the final examinations at the Goethe Institut, I would very much appreciate it if you would kindly write a letter of recommendation on my behalf.

I enclose a stamped envelope addressed to Herr Gilde, the personnel manager at Trans-World.

Yours sincerely,

Emily Goodman

a) *Why has Emily Goodman particularly chosen Mr Gordon as a referee?*
b) *What does she want him to do with the recommendation?*

*Letter 18.3*
## *A letter of recommendation*

PRIVATE AND **CONFIDENTIAL\***

Dear Mr Piggot,

I am very happy to provide you with the information you requested regarding Mary Stevens. This information is, however, to be kept confidential.

Miss Stevens first worked with us as a general secretary and became secretary to the Overseas Sales Manager in 1987. She proved herself to be competent, hard-working and **trustworthy\***.

I feel sure that she will prove herself to be an ideal employee if you decide to offer her the position she seeks.

Yours sincerely,

Michael Stroth,
Managing Director

a) On what condition does Mr Stroth agree to provide information about Mary Stevens?

b) What did she eventually become when she worked for Mr Stroth?

*Exercise 18*

*Write a letter to a Italian company who have asked you for a reference concerning Miss Jackson. She has applied to them for the post of Assistant to the Export Manager. Mention that:*

- she entered your service 5 years ago as a trainee secretary.
- she continually tried to improve herself professionally by taking evening courses in secretarial practice, Italian and electronic communications.
- a year ago, she became Personal Assistant to the Sales Manager.
- part of her work now is to deal with all overseas correspondence.
- you are persuaded that she would be a most suitable person for the post.

Study the model letters, answer the questions and complete the exercises.

*Letter 19.1*
*Covering letter with literature and samples*

Dear Sirs,

Please find enclosed the latest literature and samples
of our new range. I have also included a **display\* kit\***
for your window or **counter\*** which you may want to test
out at your **premises\*** in Reims.

You will find additional information on prices,
**discounts\*, incentives\*** and marketing materials for
your sales staff.

I hope all goes well and look forward to extra orders
in the near future.

Yours faithfully,


James Martin,
Publicity Manager


Encl:

a) What does **Encl**: *refer to?*
b) What other means does James Martin use to promote sales?

## Letter 19.2
### Covering letter for an illustrated brochure presenting new products

Dear Mr Simpson,

Further[1] to your telephone call last week, I am sending
you our illustrated brochure of the range of micro-wave
ovens **featuring\*** 10 cooking speeds, touch-sensitive
controls and an automatically cleaned base with a
special browning **adapter\***.

For 1992 we have introduced additional colours for the
popular Speedy range, these now being **available\*** in the
following colours:

- white
- clear blue
- metallic grey
- red

The ovens illustrated are just part of what very many
of our customers consider to be the largest range of
micro-wave ovens available in one catalogue – all from
high- grade manufacturers whose quality controls are
**renowned\* throughout\*** the country.

Assuring you of my best services and personal attention
at all times.

Yours sincerely,


G. Lemercier,
Vice President

---

[1] following, adding to


a) *What are the special characteristics of these micro-wave ovens?*
b) *How does Mr Lemercier try to convince his customer that his products are the best?*

## Letter 19.3
### *Announcing the **acquisition**\* of a new company*

Dear Sirs,

We have pleasure in informing you that we have
purchased the business of Sunnyside Travel in Dover.

There will be no change in the name or policies of the
company, which has proved to be extremely successful in
the past. Indeed, we shall make every effort to
**maintain**\* the **tradition**\* of quality service for which
the previous owner was well known.

As owners of Dover Travel, we are very familiar with
the travel business and also have **adequate**\* **resources**\*
to conduct the affairs of our newly acquired company
**efficiently**\*.

We hope that you will offer us an opportunity to prove
that Sunnyside Travel is able to provide the same up-
to-date service as before.

Yours faithfully,

John Carrington
**Proprietor**\*

a) *What was the previous owner well known for?*
b) *What is the writer's present position?*

### Exercise 19

*Write a letter from an agent informing a German company that you are about to open an agency for high-pressure cleaning pumps. Tell them that:*

- your connection with the leading manufacturers allows you to offer goods at competitive prices.
- in addition, your Hamburg office is organized to locate and supply goods that are not available on the German market.
- they should not hesitate to place a trial order by sending the attached form.
- you give a reduction of 15% on all orders received before the end of the year.

# Hotel Reservations

*Study the model letters, answer the questions and complete the exercises.*

*Letter 20.1*
*Making reservations (1)*

Dear Sirs,

Please reserve a single room for our Sales Manager for
7, 8 & 9 March.

He will be arriving at about 5 p.m. on the 7th and will
leave mid-morning on the 10th.

He would appreciate it if you could book him a room at
the back of the hotel.

Yours faithfully,


Phyllis Philips
Secretary

a) *How long will the sales manager be staying at the hotel?*
b) *Where in the hotel would he like his room?*

*Letter 20.2*
*Making reservations (2)*

Dear Sirs,

As our Overseas Sales Manager will be visiting Paris in
July for the Soft Furnishings Trade Fair, he will
require a small **suite*** and **access*** to a conference
room. A single room will also be needed for his
secretary on the same floor.

I would appreciate it if you could let me know by
return[1] if you can reserve this **accommodation*** from 12
to 16 July **inclusive***. Could you also let us have
details of your charges.

Yours faithfully,


Mary Stewart,
per pro[2] Mr Jackson,
Sales Manager

[1] by the next post
[2] per procurationem (pp) - on behalf of, in the place of


a) *What kind of accommodation does the Sales Manager require?*
b) *What information has Ms Stewart asked for?*

Letter 20.3
*Confirming a reservation*

Dear Mr Brooks,

I am writing to confirm your reservation for a single
room with bath for 12 - 15 July. The room will be
available after 12.30 p.m. on the 12th.

As you are arriving by air, you may like to take
advantage of[1] our Airport **Shuttle\*** Service. Our minibus
leaves Terminal 3 every hour on the half hour, and the
service is free for guests of the hotel.

Yours sincerely,


Jill Evans,
Manageress

[1] make use of

a) *What kind of accommodation has been reserved?*
b) *How can Mr Brooks get from the airport to the hotel?*

*Exercise 20*

*Write a letter to the manager of a hotel in London to say that you will
be coming to the city from 1 March to 6 March. Inform him that you
would:*

- like to book 2 single rooms and 2 double rooms with
  showers for six nights.
- like breakfast in your rooms but will take dinner in the
  main dining room in the evenings.
- appreciate it if you could have the same room at the back
  of the hotel as you had last year as the rooms overlooking
  the street are rather noisy.
- say also that your group will arrive at Heathrow at about
  11 a.m.
- but as you have meetings until the early evening, you will
  probably check in just in time for dinner at about 7 p.m.
- end by saying that you look forward to an early confirmation
  so that you can complete arrangements for the visit.

# PART THREE
## RECALL EXERCISES

# Recall exercises

*Complete the following by adding ONE word in each space:*

## Unit 1 — Requests for information

*Letter 1.1*
Dear Mr Godart, We acknowledge ......... of your brochure ......... the new ......... in your Weedolex .......... We would be very ......... if you would let us have ......... details of your ......... Yours .........,

*Letter 1.2*
Dear Mr Jones, We have been ......... attracted by the ......... -wheel locks, model X3/27 on page 43 of your .......... Could you ......... let us know if you are in ......... ......... to deliver .........? Yours .........,

*Letter 1.3*
Dear Sirs, We were very ......... to receive your ......... of 8th June announcing the ......... of your new ......... jacks. Could possibly send us the address of the ......... for our .........? Yours faithfully,

*Letter 1.4*
Dear Sirs, We would like to ......... your special ......... of coats to our silk and woollens ......... business. We would be ......... if you would send us your ......... price list and let us know your ......... for .......... Yours faithfully, Janet Watkins, Overseas Sales ..........

## Unit 2 — Acknowledging an enquiry

*Letter 2.1*
Dear Sir, Following your ........., please find enclosed an illustrated ......... presenting our SELTEK .......... In ......... of receiving your order, we ........., Yours ........., Jack Kenyon, Export ......... Manager.

*Letter 2.2*
Dear Mr Bronson, With ......... to your letter of 25th January, 1991, we have ......... in sending you our ......... catalogue. We are quite ......... to send you all further ......... information. We thank you for your .......... Yours ........., Frederick Page, Overseas Sales ..........

*Letter 2.3*
Dear Madam, We thank you very much for your ......... in our Purtex ......... - aluminium ......... for ......... catering and frozen food - sizes A1 & A5. Our ......... will supply you with all ......... information and will advise you on the ......... of trays that will suit your particular .......... Yours faithfully, Gordon Williams, Manager.

*Letter 2.4*
Dear Sir, We have received your ......... of 10 August in which you ......... details of our range of bottles, boxes and wide-necked ......... for the ......... of food products, medicines and toiletries. Please ......... enclosed our latest ......... as well as a list of prices currently in .......... We look ......... to receiving your order in the very near ..........

## Unit 3 — Placing orders

*Letter 3.1*

Dear Sirs, ......... having examined your ......... presenting your water-cooled ......... saws, we would like to ......... an order for: 100 Code No. 900 54200 diameter thickness 230 mm, cutting thickness 2.2 mm. 250 Code No. 900 54200 diameter thickness 300 mm, cutting thickness 3.2 mm. Hoping that this will ......... the beginning of a continuing ......... between our two companies, we remain, Yours faithfully, Henry Pierce, Export Manager.

*Letter 3.2*

Dear Mr Collins, ......... having examined the catalogue that you ......... sent us, we have ......... in sending you ......... an order for trouser skirts, ......... 95 cm, on a straight belt mounting with ......... and buttons. 50 maroon, sizes 36, 38, 40: 50 black, sizes 42, 44, 46: Please send the ......... by air. Yours ........., John Wilkins.

*Letter 3.3*

Dear Sir, We have received your ......... of 5th of December. We now have the ......... of sending you the enclosed order for 30 ......... of step ladders with top ........., aluminium steps and a supporting ......... in the open position. Reference:32.145, etc. Please arrange ......... by train. Yours ........., George Pattison,

*Letter 3.4*

Dear Sir, Following our telephone ......... of 10 May ........., we are ordering: 15 non-return valves, etc. Please send the ......... by normal ......... service. Hoping that you will ......... the order with your ......... care. Yours ........., Freddy Macdonald.

## Unit 4 — Dealing with orders

*Letter 4.1*

We thank you for your ......... No. 321/4-9, for:- 200 kg of "Kenya" 1 (coffee) quality No. 493 ......... £4.50/kilo. The ......... will be sent today ......... rail. Yours faithfully, Dave Burbridge, Sales ..........

*Letter 4.2*

Dear Sir, Thank for your ......... of 4th November and for the ......... order. We will let you know ......... we will be able to confirm ......... of the goods. We thank you ......... more for your .......... Yours faithfully, Thomas Hamilton, Sales Manager.

*Letter 4.3*

Dear Sir, I have ......... in acknowledging ......... of your order of the 15th ......... regarding: the aluminium sheeting, the polyethylene ........., the ......... folders. We have all the ......... in stock and everything ......... be ......... for ......... next week. Yours faithfully, Greg Dodgson, Sales Manager.

*Letter 4.4*

Dear Madam, We are ......... to inform you ......... your order No. 264/3613 of 6 June is in .......... The ......... will arrive ......... the end of the month. We would be ......... if you would inform us ......... the ......... arrive. Hoping that this ......... is acceptable, we remain, Yours faithfully, Harold Fielding, Export Department.

## Unit 5 — Packing and transport

*Letter 5.1*

Dear Sir, Following our ......... No. A/9753 of 5th February, we have to ......... out that the 20 ......... of triple mirrors 140 - EQUINOXE 8490 must be delivered with ......... lighting, ......... and switches to our Hull .......... On the other ........., order No. 867/343 must be sent to our ......... in Bremen. The mirrors should be in bales ......... in sacking with metal ..........

In ......... of your future orders to which we shall always give the ......... care, we remain, Yours faithfully,

*Letter 5.2*
Dear Sirs, We have received your letter of 5th January. The ......... will be sent to your ......... in Rotterdam according to your ......... as soon as ........... All the ......... are clearly ......... with the accepted international sign - ......... - top - bottom. We thank you for your order. Yours faithfully, Gordon Barnes, Director of Overseas Sales.

*Letter 5.3*
Dear Sirs, ......... your letter of 8th August, please find enclosed the ......... concerning the ......... of our order No. A/765. Each ......... must be packed in ......... cases to avoid all ......... of damage during .......... Please deliver the goods to our shipper's ......... and send the invoice ......... duplicate.

*Letter 5.4*
Dear Madam, As you ......... in your letter of 8th March, we are sending you 20 50 kg cases of ......... snails ......... refrigerated ......... to Boulogne from the ......... of Dover. We hope that they will arrive ......... and in good ........., that you will appreciate the ......... of our ......... and that we shall have the ......... to do ......... with you again. Yours faithfully, Gerald Moss, Director.

## Unit 6 — Confirmation of delivery

*Letter 6.1*
Dear Sir, We have received the trial order consisting ......... the ......... -mentioned articles which arrived ......... perfect condition. If, as we hope, our customers like your suntan products, we shall be pleased order larger amounts ......... you. Yours faithfully, James Willis, Managing Director.

*Letter 6.2*
Dear Sir, We thank you for your ......... of 26th June which arrived this morning ......... the time required and in good .......... The ......... and the goods ......... perfectly. We hope to be in a ......... to send you an ......... order shortly. Yours faithfully, Janice Green, Director.

*Letter 6.3*
Dear Sir, We are ......... to confirm the arrival of after-shave ......... Samarkand (No 1) and Jamaïque (No 3) ......... we ordered two weeks ......... (Nos 210 & 11 of our ......... No. 3692). Our ......... collected the ......... from the ......... yesterday. In ......... of the items which have ......... to be delivered, we remain, Yours faithfully, Sylvia Witty, Sales Director.

*Letter 6.4*
Dear Madam, The ......... part of the ......... of wall ......... has just arrived by rail. We are ......... to confirm that the first ......... delivered ......... perfectly with the ......... note. You can expect a ......... order from us .......... Yours faithfully, John Reynolds, Import Manager

## Unit 7 — Complaints

*Letter 7.1*
Dear Sir, We have just taken ......... of the ......... in our order No. 143/2A. We regret to inform you that the bathroom cabinets (with mirror, ......... lighting and shelf, etc.) are not ......... to the usual standard. Could you please make the necessary ......... for the replacement of these articles and their .........? In ......... of a speedy ........., we remain, Yours faithfully, George Kennett, Manager.

*Letter 7.2*
Dear Sir, We regret to inform you that our ......... of a set of weight-training ......... was

delivered to us in a very bad .......... You can understand our .......... We are now returning the ......... items and would be ......... if you would replace them .......... Yours faithfully, John Goddard.

*Letter 7.3*
Dear Sir, We acknowledge ......... of the ......... pine settees which you sent to us ......... to our order of the 5th .......... Although the boxes are ........., when we unpacked them, we discovered that a certain ......... of the items were broken. We have told the ......... about the damage and kept the boxes and their ......... so that they may be .......... Yours faithfully, Mervyn Little.

*Letter 7.4*
Dear Sirs, Your ......... was at last delivered yesterday from the air ......... depot. ........., I regret to have to inform you that the goods were ......... damaged. I would ......... be obliged if you would send your ......... as soon as ......... so that he can verify the .......... himself. Yours faithfully, Mark Picard, Managing Director.

## Unit 8 — Apologies and replies to complaints

*Letter 8.1*
Dear Sirs, In ......... to your letter of 3rd March on the ......... of the non-......... of the wine glasses, we have asked our Shipping Department and they ......... us that the goods ......... ......... by the storm we had in this area last week. You can rest assured that we shall make ......... that this order will be dealt with as ......... as ......... Please accept our ......... for the .......... Yours faithfully, George Eastern, Sales Manager

*Letter 8.2*
Dear Miss Colley, We very much regret that ......... now we have not been ......... to send you the computer disk labels you ordered. We ......... have them in ........., but cannot ......... any invoice in your name. Can you, in order to help us with our ........., send us the number and the ......... of your order? We assure you that we shall give the ......... our ......... attention ......... we receive your .......... Yours faithfully, Peter Derrick.

*Letter 8.3*
Dear Sirs, We have noticed that we have ......... you by £400 and you will find a ......... note attached for that .......... We are in the ......... of changing computers, which has led to a certain ......... of ......... of invoices. As ......... as things are ......... to normal, we hope to be able to continue as .......... Please accept our .......... Yours faithfully,

*Letter 8.4*
Dear Madam, We are very ......... out to hear that the wooden spring bed frames which we sent you by train became ......... during ......... and consequently arrived .......... We offer our most ......... excuses for this ......... which was caused by the ......... of a new packer. We are ready to accept full ......... for the damage and we have immediately ......... the articles. Please excuse us for all the ......... that this may have ......... you. Yours faithfully, Howard Midwinter, Dispatch Dept.

## Unit 9 — Complaints and replies about payment

*Letter 9.1*
Dear Mr Cherrau, We would like to draw your ......... to our bill of 4th March. ......... we have not yet received your ......... for the last two ........., we would be very ......... if you would send it as ......... as possible. I am ......... that this delay is due to an ......... in your ......... department and while awaiting ........., I remain, Yours faithfully, A Littlejohn, Sales Director.

*Letter 9.2*
Dear Sirs, We wish to remind you that your ......... No. 896/1A dated 8 August has not yet been .......... We ask you to give this ......... your most ......... attention. If you have ......... transferred the ......... in question, please take no notice of this .......... We look ......... to receiving your ......... letter. Yours ........., Ronald Bates, ......... pro The Managing Director.

*Letter 9.3*
Dear Madam, We have received your letter of 12 September ......... in which you draw our ........., to the ......... that we have ......... the time limit of your ......... two bills. As we are experiencing temporary .........-flow ........., we are sending you half of the ......... as an ......... and we shall pay the ......... ......... the next three months. We are very grateful for your .......... Yours faithfully, Jeremy Milton.

*Letter 9.4*
Dear Sirs, I have ......... received your letter of 8th January concerning the ......... of our ......... A/97867. As you are ........., our ......... has always been to settle our ......... with the minimum of .......... However, the ......... caused by the hurricane in the South of England resulted in ......... cash-......... problems and we would be very ......... if you would allow us 30 days .......... Thanking you in .......... Yours faithfully, Percival Davey, Accounts Department.

## Unit 10 — Status enquiries

*Letter 10.1*
Dear Sir, We have just received an ......... order from the company ......... name you will find enclosed. Could you please let us have full ......... on this company's ......... position. We would ......... like to know if this company enjoys a ......... financial ......... and if we can let them have ......... up to a credit ......... of DM 50 000. You can rest assured that this ......... will be kept strictly .......... Yours faithfully, Donald Spencer, General Manager.

*Letter 10.2*
Dear Sirs, We would be very ......... if we could obtain ......... about Carlton Incorporated, Seattle, Washington, USA, who would like to open an ......... and who have given us your name as a .......... We know that you often have business ......... with them, so we thought that you, ......... than anyone else, could give us ......... about their ......... situation. Do you think that we could ......... do business with them? In the ......... of a speedy reply, we enclose an international ......... coupon. Yours faithfully, Milton Jackson, Export Manager.

*Letter 10.3*
Dear Sirs, We would like to know your ......... on the ......... of the Wadja company in Budapest, ......... have given your name as a .......... Before ......... committing ........., we would be obliged if you would give us your ......... on the ......... of their work and of their ......... sales service. We assure you that all ......... that you give us will be treated .......... Yours faithfully, Irene St John, Manageress.

*Letter 10.4*
Dear Sirs, Baker Jackson plc have contacted us with a ......... to placing an ......... order for household .......... They have given us your ......... and ......... and we would ......... be very ......... if you would supply us with ......... on their ......... situation as soon as ......... ......... we are sure of their ......... to pay, we would like ......... that their financial situation guarantees quarterly ......... payments of up to $50 000. ......... to say, that all ......... will remain .......... Yours faithfully, Jack Funnel, Sales Director.

## Unit 11 — Cancellations and alterations

*Letter 11.1*
Dear Sir, We are obliged to inform you that a ......... has slipped into our order No. A/147B of 5 October last. ......... of: Storage case for 18 compact disks, it should read: Storage box for 10 audio cassettes. ......... excuse us for this ......... ......... Yours faithfully, Jurgen Zimmerman, Shipping Department.

*Letter 11.2*
Dear Sirs, On 4 January we ordered a graphic ......... VOXIMOND ......... should be delivered at the end of the month. We have, ........., discovered that our ......... stock is ......... for the ......... month and we would like to cancel the .......... I hope that, in ......... of our .........-standing ......... with you, you will accept this .......... Yours faithfully,

*Letter 11.3*
Dear Sir, We regret to learn from your ......... of 9 October that it is ......... for you to fulfil our order No. 875-326 ......... to the stipulated .......... We have to remind you ......... we insisted the ......... date should be adhered to and now see ......... obliged to cancel the order. Yours faithfully, William Ferry, Sales Manager.

*Letter 11.4*
Dear Madam, ......... you have not got these ......... in ........., we would be obliged if you would cancel our ......... of batches of 8 pairs of half-socks and replace it with batches of 10 pairs of half-stockings (colour the ......... as the half-socks). Please find enclosed a ......... order form. We should be obliged ......... you would confirm as ......... as ......... that this change is .......... We hope to receive a ......... ........., Yours faithfully, Claire Conroy, Chief Buyer.

## Unit 12 — Introducing a new salesperson

*Letter 12.1*
Dear Mr Chilananda, We have ......... in announcing the ......... of our new ........., Brian Rothwell, to Bangkok with a complete ......... of our new .......... He will call on you ......... the ......... of next week. I am ......... that you will find Mr Rothwell both ......... and obliging, and that you will appreciate his ......... qualities. I hope that you will offer him a warm ......... in Bangkok and place some ........., which will receive our ......... attention, Yours ........., John Philips, Managing Director.

*Letter 12.2*
Dear Sir, We learn with great ......... that you are interested in our type of .......... We are ......... to inform you that our ........., Duncan Shoesmith, will very ......... be in your ......... with a complete ......... of our latest ......... as well as our ......... range. We would be ......... if you would let us know as soon as possible ......... a visit is ......... so that we can arrange a .......... Yours faithfully, Harry Moss, Sales Manager.

*Letter 12.3*
Dear Sir, Our new ......... in your area, Bill Davey, will call to see you ......... the ......... of the coming week. He will inform you ......... of the ......... and time of his visit and we hope that you will offer him a warm .......... If you wish to ......... an order, you can be ......... that it will be treated with our ......... care and .......... We hope that this arrangement is ......... to you. Yours faithfully, Nicky Marchant, Overseas Sales Manager.

*Letter 12.4*
Dear Madam, We are very ......... to introduce John Higgins, our new area .......... He will show you, on our ........., a ......... of our ......... models. We would ......... like to draw your ......... to the ......... quality of the models in Nylon which sell at extremely ......... prices. We

hope that you will ......... us with an order which, it goes ......... saying, will be processed with the ......... care. Yours faithfully, Martin Goldsmith, Manager.

## Unit 13 — Insurance

*Letter 13.1 — Thanking a client for a completed proposal form and enclosing a cover note.*
Dear Sirs, We thank you for your ......... of 12 July ......... was attached to the ......... form. We are writing to inform you that our staff ......... now preparing your insurance ......... which you will receive ......... now and the ......... of the .......... In the ........., you are, of course, covered. Please find the ......... note enclosed. Yours faithfully, Jeremy Baines, Chief ..........

*Letter 13.2 — Asking for compensation from a supplier for damaged goods.*
Dear Sirs, We regret to inform you that ......... of the goods sent by our ......... in St. Malo on the ......... ship "Lincoln" arrived in a very bad .......... Please find enclosed a ......... from the ......... Officials. You will notice that they estimate the ......... to be £500. The cargo was ......... insured against all ......... by our Hull office. We request you to accept the ......... as evaluated by your own ......... and settle the ......... at an ......... date. Yours faithfully, George Page.

*Letter 13.3 — Requesting indemnity from a shipper for damaged goods.*
Dear Sirs, When your containers ......... in Hamburg ......... lorry this morning, the shipping agents noticed that several of the boxes in your consignment ......... ......... damaged. On being notified about the ........., we ......... ordered our ......... to examine the cargo. The articles are ......... but some of them have been spoilt, for example: 2 antique walnut tables, etc. Please find ......... the assessor's report in ......... as well as a ......... from the ......... agent confirming that the ......... was noticed ......... the lorry arrived at the depot. We would appreciate it ......... you would get in touch with the ......... about the problem. The insurance ......... number is P/96106. In the ........., we would be ......... if you would replace the ......... goods mentioned ......... as we have customers awaiting .......... Yours faithfully, J. Laurence.

## Unit 14 — Appointing agents

*Letter 14.1 — Offering an agency*
Dear Sirs, We have been selling a ......... quantity of English ......... to different ......... of France and are interested in appointing an .......... to explore the ......... and develop the ......... further. The products in ......... are a wide ......... of jams and honey. Your name was suggested as agent by Pommet Frères of Dijon, and on their ........., we would like to offer you the ......... agency for France. Goods will be consigned to you ......... to your instructions ......... we are only ......... with the tastes and particular ......... of customers in the north-east and realize that these must ......... from region to region. We are enclosing our price list which will give you some ......... of the varieties we produce. Since we realize the ......... of introducing a new product to ......... buyers, we are willing to pay a ......... of 15% on ......... sales. We are sure that this ......... will be mutually ......... and hope that you will accept our offer. We would very much ......... an early reply, so that we can prepare our introductory ......... in good time. Yours faithfully,

*Letter 14.2 — Accepting the offer of an agency*
Dear Mr Wilson, Thank you for your ......... of 7 February offering us an ......... for your potted meats. We would be ......... to accept the offer. We must ......... out, however, that only a ......... agency would be ......... as the ......... for your potted meats here is ......... limited because of local .........; besides, the ......... for fresh foods here would also make it ......... to extend the market for English potted meats .......... In these ........., we feel that competition from another agent would not make our ......... worthwhile. If you give us your ......... agency for France, we feel sure that our wide marketing ......... and ......... contacts will

enable us to introduce your goods ......... in this country. Yours sincerely, Henri Biquet.

## Unit 15 — Overseas payments

*Letter 15.1*
Dear Ms Sanderson, Thank you for your ......... regarding our ......... of fire-.........
equipment. We supply such equipment ......... the world for use by ......... such as
yourselves, and will be glad to provide a large order ......... a letter of ......... issued through
a ......... international bank. We look forward, therefore, to receiving a letter of credit in
......... course, when your order will be processed in the ......... way. Yours faithfully, Phillip
Lemington, Managing Director.

*Letter 15.2 — Confirming an order against a letter of credit.*
Dear Sirs, .........: Your Order No. JK/9630. We acknowledge with thanks the ......... of the
above order. We are in the ......... of preparing the magnetic white display boards for
shipment. Our agent has ......... us that you will arrange ......... by Letter of Credit in our
........., valid until 30th June, 19—. These terms are ......... to us. As soon as the ......... has been
confirmed by our bank, the goods will be shipped ......... instructed. Yours faithfully, John
Wheeler, Sales Manager.

*Letter 15.3 — Advising that a letter of credit has been opened.*
Dear Sirs, With ......... to your letter of 19 March, we write to inform you that we have
instructed the Banque Nationale de Paris in Lyon to open a ......... for £5000 in your .........,
......... until 30 June, 1995. This credit will be confirmed by Barclays Bank in Guernsey and
will be issued when your ......... is received at this bank. Please make sure that all necessary
......... are attached: Bill of ......... in duplicate, 1 Customs ........., Insurance ......... for £7500.
4 ......... Commercial Invoices. Yours faithfully, Peter Horton, Chief Accountant.

## Unit 16 — Job applications

*Letter 16.1 — Applying for a job (1)*
Dear Sirs, I wish to apply for the ......... of bilingual secretary at AGCOM Ltd., as ......... in
the "Times" on Monday, 5 October, 1988. The attached ......... gives details of my
career and ......... up to this moment, which in ......... are as follows: Since ......... a B.A. in
1982, I have successfully ......... part-time courses in French and German. For the past 6
years I have been a private secretary in the Overseas Sales department at Selby Ltd., with
particular ......... for all overseas .......... During this time I have successfully ......... a
completely new ......... system and modernized the whole office .......... Having worked
......... at this level for some time, I now wish to seek further ......... in this field and would
like to ......... up the challenge of a new .......... I would be grateful, therefore, if you would
allow me the ......... of meeting with you and your colleagues to discuss my .......... Yours
faithfully, Kathleen O'Houlihan.

*Letter 16.2 — Applying for a job (2)*
Dear Mr Trulle, Having ......... for the past four years as the only secretary in a ......... small
business, I would like to ......... ......... the post of ......... secretary as advertised in "The
Guardian" on Tuesday, 12 January, 19—. As ......... secretary to the ......... of James Young
plc in Southampton, I was not only ......... ......... the day to day running of the office, but for
all overseas ........., mostly in Spanish and Portuguese as we exported to many South
American countries. I was also ......... for the more personal work of ......... private
appointments, ......... telephone calls and visitors and ......... Mr Young's paperwork and
correspondence. With the above ......... behind me, I am thoroughly ......... with the duties
of an ......... secretary and believe that I will certainly ......... up to all your expectations. I
enclose my CV and would be grateful if you would ......... me the opportunity to discuss
my ......... with you in person. I would be happy to attend an interview at your ........., and

can be reached on my ......... at 01-671 986. Yours sincerely, Jeremy Hinchcliffe.

## Unit 17 — Replies to job applications

*Letter 17.1 — Calling an applicant for interview.*
Dear Miss Billings, Thank you for your letter ......... for the ......... of secretary. I shall be ......... if you could come here for an ......... on Wednesday next, 13 March, at 2.30 p.m. If that day or time is not ......... for you, I would appreciate it ......... you could ......... my secretary know, and I will try to ......... the interview for a date and time that is ......... for both of us. Yours sincerely, Peter Dodgson, ......... Manager.

*Letter 17.2 — Confirmation of employment*
Dear Mr Jackson, With ......... to your letter of Monday 12 January, I am pleased to confirm the ......... of a ......... as systems analyst in this company. Enclosed are three copies of our ......... of .......... Please sign two of ......... and return them to my ......... as ......... as possible. We have also enclosed a leaflet ......... you full details of our ......... fund, our luncheon ......... scheme, the sports club and the annual .......... If you have any ......... about the terms of the contract ........., please do not ......... to contact me. Yours sincerely, Rosemary Giggins, Director.

*Letter 17.3 — Turning down an applicant after interview*
Dear Mr Fish, Thank you for your ......... visit regarding .......... After considerable deliberation ......... the light ......... our conversation last week, I have come to the ......... that we cannot at ......... offer you ......... at our offices. As I mentioned when we met, I will keep your ......... on file for future ......... as we regularly look for extra or ......... staff. I am glad you came and explained your ......... so well, and hope that you do not find this decision too .......... Yours sincerely, Donald Hobson, Recruitment.

## Unit 18 — Personal references

*Letter 18.1 — Asking permission to give a person's name as referee.*
Dear Mr Aubert, I am ......... to apply for the ......... of Sales ......... at Jack Rothwell & Co. in Madrid. I would very much ......... it if I could ......... your name in my list of .......... As you are ......... with my work with Llama Gabilondo y Cia, S.A., you will be able to give Jack Rothwell a fair ......... of my .......... I enclose a stamped, addressed .......... for your reply. Yours sincerely, John Bridges.

*Letter 18.2 — Asking a referee to send a reference directly to a potential employer.*
Dear Mr. Gordon, I am applying for the position of ......... secretary with Trans-World Travel in Heidelberg. As you gave me every ......... to continue with my study of German and helped me prepare ......... the final examinations at the Goethe Institut, I would very much appreciate it if you would ......... write a letter of ......... on my behalf. I enclose a stamped envelope, ......... to Herr Gilde , the ......... manager at Trans-World. Yours sincerely, Emily Goodman.

*Letter 18.3 - A letter of recommendation.*
PRIVATE AND .........
Dear Mr Piggot, I am very ......... to provide you with the ......... you requested ......... Mary Stevens. This ......... is, however, to be kept .......... Miss Stevens first worked with us as a ......... secretary and became secretary ......... to the Overseas Sales Manager in 1987. She ......... herself to be competent, .........-working and trustworthy. I feel ......... that she will prove ......... to be an ......... employee if you decide to offer her the ......... she seeks. Yours sincerely, Michael Stroth, Managing Director.

## Unit 19 — Sales letters

*Letter 19.1 — Covering letter with literature and samples.*
Dear Sirs, Please find enclosed the ......... literature and ......... of our new ......... I have also included a ......... kit for your window or ......... which you may want to test out at your ......... in Reims. You will find ......... information on prices, discounts, incentives and marketing ......... for your sales .......... I hope all goes well and look ......... to extra orders in the ......... future. Yours faithfully,

*Letter 19.2 — Covering letter for an illustrated brochure.*
Dear Mr Simpson, ......... to your telephone ......... last week, I am sending you our illustrated ......... of the ......... of micro-wave ovens ......... 10 cooking speeds, touch-......... controls and an automatically cleaned base with a special browning .......... For 1992 we have introduced ......... colours for the ......... "Speedy" range, these now being ......... in the following colours: white, clear blue, metallic grey, red. The ovens illustrated are just ......... of what many of our ......... consider to be the ......... range of micro-wave ovens ......... in one catalogue - all from high-grade ......... whose quality ......... are renowned ......... the country. Assuring you of my best services and ......... attention at all times. Yours faithfully, G. Lemercier, Vice President.

*Letter 19.3 — Announcing the acquisition of a new company.*
Dear Sirs, We have ......... in informing you that we have purchased the ......... of Sunnyside Travel in Dover. There will be no ......... in the name or ......... of the company which has proved to be ......... successful in the .......... Indeed, we shall make every ......... to maintain the ......... of quality service for which the ......... owner was well known. As ......... of Dover Travel, we are very ......... with the travel business and also have ......... resources to conduct the ......... of our newly acquired company .......... We hope that you will offer us an ......... to prove that Sunnyside Travel is able to provide the same ......... service as before. Yours faithfully, John Carrington, Proprietor.

## Unit 20 — Hotel reservations

*Letter 20.1 — Making reservations (1)*
Dear Sirs, Please ......... a single room for our Sales Manager for 7, 8 & 9 March. He will be arriving at ......... 5 p.m. on the 7th and will ......... mid-morning on the 10th. He ......... appreciate it if you could book him a room ......... the back of the hotel. Yours faithfully, Phyllis Philips.

*Letter 20.2 — Making reservations (2)*
Dear Sirs, As our Overseas Sales Manager will be ......... Paris ......... July for the Soft Furnishings Trade Fair, he will ......... a small suite and ......... to a conference room. A single room will also ......... ......... for his secretary ......... the same floor. I would appreciate it if you could let me know by ......... if you can reserve this ......... from 12 to 16 July .......... Could you also let us have ......... of your .......... Yours faithfully, Mary Stewart, per pro Mr Jackson, Sales Manager.

*Letter 20.3 — Confirming a reservation.*
Dear Mr Brooks, I am writing to ......... your ......... for a single room with bath for 12 - 15 July. The room will be ......... after 12.30 p.m. on the 12th. ......... you are arriving by air, you may like to take ......... of our Airport ......... Service. Our ......... leaves Terminal 3 every hour ......... the half hour, and the ......... is free for ......... of the hotel. Yours sincerely, Jill Evans, Manageress.

UNIT 1 - *Requests for information*

*Letter 1.1*

a)  He sent him a brochure.
b)  He wants further details of his products.

*Letter 1.2*

a)  He found out about it from the brochure.
b)  To ask if the company can deliver direct from the factory.
c)  The familiar greeting, **Dear Mr Jones**.

*Letter 1.3*

a)  The purpose was to give information about the launching of a new product.
b)  No, he doesn't, he wants to buy from a local dealer.

*Letter 1.4*

a)  By including a special range of coats.
b)  She requires a current price list and the conditions for delivery overseas.
c)  She is the Manager in charge of overseas sales.

*Drills*

1)
a)  I acknowledge reception of your brochure on 10th August presenting your new prices.
b)  We acknowledge reception of your delivery schedules on 8th February presenting your enlarged network.
c)  The directors acknowledge reception of your draft plans on 21st March presenting your modernization project.
d)  Our client acknowledges reception of your software on 30th November presenting your new filing system.

2)
a)  Our clients would be very grateful if you would let us have a statement of account.
b)  We would be very much obliged if you would let us have an up dated price list.
c)  I would be very grateful if you would let me have any special requests.
d)  Mr Jackson would be very much obliged if you would let him have a pro forma invoice.

3)
a)  Your circular has attracted my attention and I am particularly interested in your tool kits presented on page 54.
b)  Your leaflets have attracted Mrs Field's attention and she is particularly interested in your sports clothes presented on page 72.
c)  Your up-to-date list has attracted my attention and I am particularly interested in your price changes presented on page 44.

d) The brochure has attracted Mr Clarke's attention and he is particularly interested in your range of dinner services presented on page 67.

*Exercise 1.1*

Dear Sir, We acknowledge reception of your brochure and we would like add to our business your range of blow moulding machines. We would be very much obliged if you would send us further details on this range as well as your conditions for overseas delivery. In addition, would it be possible to let us know if you could deliver direct? Yours faithfully,

*Exercise 1.2*

Dear Sirs, I acknowledge reception of your letter of 9th January and I am particularly interested in your new range of windbreaker jackets. I would be obliged if you could let me have your latest price list as well as your conditions for overseas delivery. Yours faithfully,

*Exercise 1.3*

Dear Sirs, I acknowledge reception of your letter of 9 January and I am particularly interested in your new range of tooth-brushes. I would be obliged if you would let me have your current price list and the name and address of a distributor in my area. Yours faithfully,

## UNIT 2 - *Acknowledging an enquiry*

*Letter 2.1*

a) Mrs Schwartzkopf did.
b) It refers to an illustrated folder.
c) They produce optical measuring instruments.

*Letter 2.2*

a) The writer asked for a catalogue.
b) The familiar greeting, 'Dear Mr Bronson'.

*Letter 2.3*

a) They are sizes of aluminium trays.
b) She prepares and sells pre-cooked frozen food.
c) Because he is sending a representative.

*Letter 2.4*

a) It requested details of the company's products.
b) Containers for food, medicine and toiletries.
c) The current Sarrabia price list.
d) Enc: or Encl: - "Enclosures"

*Drills*

1)
a) Following Mr Norman's letter, please find enclosed an updated quotation.
b) Following my inquiry, please find enclosed my outline proposals.
c) Following our request, please find enclosed an application form.

d) Following my 'phone call, please find enclosed details of the orders outstanding.

2)
a) With reference to your letter of 4 April, I have pleasure in sending you details of the building permit.
b) With reference to your letter of 6th February, the partners have pleasure in sending you an introductory offer.
c) With reference to your letter of 13th August, the Customers' Accounts Dept has pleasure in sending you a statement.
d) With reference to your letter of 28th June, the company has pleasure in sending you a credit note.

3)
a) Please find enclosed our proposed conditions as well as an outline contract.
b) Please find enclosed an order form as well as samples of our pocket files.
c) Please find enclosed the plans as well as a preliminary agreement.
d) Please find enclosed our free coloured brochure as well as a few samples of our pull-out folders.

*Exercise 2.1*

Dear Mr Smith, We thank you for your letter of 5th March. Our Sales Manager will be sending you all further supplementary information as well as a list of prices currently in force. We look forward to receiving your order in the near future. Yours faithfully, John Birchfield.

*Exercise 2.2*

Dear Mr Skinner, We thank you for your interest in software. We are willing to send you all supplementary information. In anticipation of receiving your order, we remain, Yours faithfully,

*Exercise 2.3*

Dear Sir, With reference to your letter of 13 May, please find enclosed our most up-to-date samples as well as our latest price list. In anticipation of receiving your order, we remain, Yours faithfully,

*UNIT 3 - Placing orders*

*Letter 3.1*

a) It makes water-cooled circular saws.
c) Because Mr. Pierce hopes that his order will mark the beginning of continuing relationship.

*Letter 3.2*

a) Because the letter begins 'Dear Mr Collins'.
b) Yes, he wants it sent by air.

*Letter 3.3*

a) It's a shop selling hardware and tools.
b) They'll have to go to the railway station.

*Letter 3.4*

a) He had a telephone conversation with the supplier.
b) He want them sent by normal cargo service.
c) Because he uses the phrase 'with your usual care'.

*Drills*

1)
a) After having examined the catalogue presenting your merchandise, I would like to place an order for 50 table services, model "Savoy".
b) After having examined the circular presenting your merchandise we would like to place an order for 150 shoe racks - size 57 x 21 cm.
c) After having examined the brochure presenting your merchandise, I would like to place an order for 30 'Multi-Spark' electric gas lighters.
d) After having examined the leaflet presenting your merchandise, we would like to place an order for 20 9V digital kitchen scales.

2)
a) After having examined the list you sent me, I have pleasure in sending you herewith an order for 20 super compact sewing machines.
b) After having examined the samples you sent us, we have pleasure in sending you herewith an order for 5 programmable automatic clothes driers .
c) After having examined the brochure you sent me, I have pleasure in sending you 35 rolls of wall-to-wall carpeting.
d) After having examined the catalogue you sent us, we have pleasure in sending you 24 'Mandi' colour televisions (for UK and Continental channels).

3)
a) I now have pleasure in sending you the enclosed order for a 'Bontempi' portable electronic organ.
b) We now have pleasure in sending you the enclosed order for 10 collapsible 'Bak-Pak' baby carriers with attached wheels.
c) Mr Jackson now has pleasure in sending you the enclosed order for 20 'Bobby' dolls in vinyl, height 40 cm, with closing eyes in the reclined position.
d) They now have pleasure in sending you the enclosed order for 20 computer disk drives DD1-2, with software.

*Exercise 3.1*

Dear Sirs, After having received the brochure you recently sent us, we have pleasure in sending you an order for 100 ignition coils CX143/2. Please arrange shipment by air. Hoping that this will mark the beginning of a continuing relationship between our two companies, I remain, Yours faithfully, Martin Lemmon.

*Exercise 3.2*

Dear Mr Hornby, After having examined the samples presenting your products, we have pleasure in sending you an order for 100 hypodermic syringes. Please arrange delivery by rail. Hoping that you will expedite this order with your usual care, I remain, Yours sincerely, Philip Latour.

*Exercise 3.3*

Dear Sir, We have received your letter of 5th June. After having examined the catalogue that you recently sent us, we have pleasure in sending you herewith order No. 234/X42 for 200 mechanical gaskets. Please expedite the goods by air. Yours faithfully, Trevor Harrison.

## UNIT 4 - Dealing with orders

*Letter 4.1*

a) Delicatess plc.
b) A chain of grocers or delicatessens.
c) He says they will be sent the same day.

*Letter 4.2*

a) It included an order.
b) He will soon be writing again to confirm that the goods have been sent.

*Letter 4.3*

a) He will be able to send them during the following week.

*Letter 4.4*

a) They will arrive before the end of the month.
b) The arrangement is that the client should inform him when the goods arrive.

*Drills*

1)
a) I have pleasure in acknowledging your order of the 15th instant regarding the computer game joy-sticks.
b) The Sales Department has pleasure in acknowledging your order of the 6th instant regarding the typewriters "Eurotype".
c) Mr Collins has pleasure in acknowledging your order of the 12th instant regarding the tailored, 100% cotton, velvet skirts.
d) We have pleasure in acknowledging your order of the 18th instant regarding the short-sleeved, striped polo-necked pullovers.

2)
a) Everything will be sent today by train.
b) The packets will be sent at the end of the week by ship.
c) The container will be sent tomorrow by road.
d) The goods will be sent at the end of the month by air.

3)
a) I have the overalls in stock and everything should be ready for shipment very soon.
b) We have the cupboards in stock and everything should be ready for shipment in a week's time.
c) Our shop has the quilts in stock and everything should be ready for shipment as soon as possible.
d) Our branch has the sanding machines in stock and everything should be ready for shipment within a few days.

*Exercise 4.1*

Dear Sirs, We thank you for your order No. 435/23/32, for 10,000 dustbin-liners in pre-cut rolls and 1000 freezer bags. We have all the articles in stock, and everything should be ready for shipment within a very few days. The goods will be sent by train. Hoping that this arrangement is acceptable, we remain, Yours faithfully,

*Exercise 4.2*

Dear Sir, We thank you for your letter of the 7th March and for the accompanying order. The containers will arrive before the end of next week. Hoping that this arrangement is acceptable, we remain, Yours faithfully, James Harrison.

*Exercise 4.3*

Dear Sir, We thank you for your letter of 12 September and for the order for 6 large tarpaulins as well as 20 plastic agricultural sheets for mulching purposes. The goods will be shipped as soon as possible. We would be grateful if you would inform us when the goods arrive. Yours faithfully,

## UNIT 5 - Packing and transport

*Letter 5.1*

a) It's from a client.
b) He's referring to an adjustable mirror with three parts.
c) It must be sent to the warehouse in Bremen.
d) He'd like them to be packed in sacking bales with metal strapping.

*Letter 5.2*

a) It's to a client.
b) The containers carry the international marking for - fragile - top - bottom.

*Letter 5.3*

a) It's from a client.
b) The letter requested details of delivery requirements.
c) He will deliver them to the shipper's warehouse.

*Letter 5.4*

a) It placed an order for edible snails.
b) By his remarks about doing business with them again.

*Drills*

1)
a) Following our order of 9th September, I have to point out that the dressing gowns (with shawl collars) must be delivered to our warehouse in Newhaven.
b) Following our letter of 5th May, the manager has to point out that the glass bookcase style Louis XV must be delivered to our office in Berlin.
c) Following our letter of 6th June, we have to point out that the children's ski suits must be delivered to our Paris branch.
d) Following our letter of 15th October, we have to point out that the zodiac sign quartz watches must be delivered to our agency in Berne.

2)
a) The musical mobiles for baby's cots will be shipped to your warehouse in Croydon

soon according to your instructions.
b)  The radio-alarm clocks will be shipped to your office in Amsterdam next week according to your instructions.
c)  The cellular telephones TD 8734 will be shipped to your branch in Jena at the end of the month according to your instructions.
d)  The shower curtains will be shipped to your depot in Paris today according to your instructions.

3)
a)  As the manageress requested in her letter of 9th October, we are sending you the woollen carpets by sea from the port of Tilbury to the Hook of Holland.
b)  As our manager requested in his letter of 7th August, we are sending the compact washing-up machines by rail from Victoria to Lyon.
c)  As they requested in their letter of 15th March, we are sending the garage swing doors by road from Birmingham to Ramsgate.
d)  As our customers requested in their letter of 3rd July, we are sending the pull-down loft stairs by air freight from Heathrow to Prague.

*Exercise 5.1*

Dear Sir, Following your order No. 87430 of 12 January, we have to point out that the plant tubs must be sent to our depot in Southampton. All the containers must be clearly marked with the accepted international sign - fragile - top - bottom. We thank you for your order. Yours faithfully,

*Exercise 5.2*

Dear Sir, We have received your letter of 9th January. The boxes will be packed in bales covered in sacking with metal strapping and will be shipped to our depot in Exeter. Hoping that you will appreciate the quality of our products and that we shall have the chance to do business with you again. Yours faithfully, Harry Hall.

*Exercise 5.3*

Dear Sirs, We have received your letter of 5th August. The goods will be sent by road to your warehouse in Madrid according to your instructions as soon as possible. We hope that they will arrive quickly and in good condition, that you will appreciate the quality of our products and that we shall have the chance to do business with you again. Yours faithfully,

## UNIT 6 - *Confirmation of delivery*

*Letter 6.1*

a)  No, it is on the trading estate.
b)  To inform Produkt Forum that they have received the trial order.
c)  He will place more orders if the products are popular with his customers.

*Letter 6.2*

a)  By the phrase 'within the required time'.
b)  The invoice.
c)  She almost certainly is.

*Letter 6.3*

a)  She has had to wait two weeks.

b) It was sent by ship.
c) No, she hasn't.

*Letter 6.4*

a) They arrived by rail.
b) He checked the items against the delivery note.
c) It refers to the wall cupboards.

*Drills*

1)
a) I have received order No. 123A consisting of the bathroom cupboards which arrived in perfect condition.
b) Our Brighton branch has received the trial order consisting of quilt covers which arrived in perfect condition.
c) They have received order No. A952 consisting of pure cotton Texas jeans which arrived in perfect condition.
d) The shipping company has received order No. 43587 consisting of air conditioners which arrived in perfect condition.

2)
a) I am happy to confirm the arrival of the windcheater which I ordered last month.
b) Our manager is happy to confirm the arrival of the Eurosport ping-pong tables which he ordered a week ago.
c) Our client is happy to confirm the arrival of the dressers (width 100 cm : height 79 cm.) which he ordered in January.
d) Our clients are happy to confirm the arrival of the multi-purpose storage bags which they ordered on 12th September.

3)
a) Our agent collected the electric drill attachments from the airport yesterday.
b) My lorry will collect the aerobic outfits from the port of Tilbury tomorrow morning.
c) My assistant will collect the electric soldering irons from the warehouse next week.
d) Our customers collected the chandeliers from the storerooms two days ago.

*Exercise 6.1*

Re: Our order No. 3265/32 - 30 video-recorders. Dear Sirs, We have received the trial order consisting of the above mentioned articles which arrived in good condition. Our van collected the goods at the railway station yesterday. We hope to be in a position to send you an identical order shortly. In anticipation of the items that have yet to be delivered, we remain, Yours faithfully, ...

*Exercise 6.2*

Dear Sir, We are happy to confirm the arrival of the armchairs which we ordered two weeks ago (Nos. 7 & 8 of our order). If, as we hope, our customers like the goods, we shall be pleased to order larger amounts from you. Yours faithfully, John Field, Chief Buyer.

*Exercise 6.3*

Dear Mr Trafford, The first part of the consignment of frozen cooked meals has just arrived. The invoice and the shipment tally perfectly. In anticipation of the goods that have yet to be delivered, we remain, Yours faithfully,

## UNIT 7 - Complaints

*Letter 7.1*

a) Yes, he has (see the order number).
b) The goods are not up to their usual standard.
c) He wants the company to replace them.

*Letter 7.2*

a) No, he isn't.
b) He wants the damaged items replaced.
c) Because he has already taken action by returning the items for immediate replacement.
d) It refers to the weight-training equipment.

*Letter 7.3*

a) When he unpacked them.
b) He has reported it to the shipper.
c) He is keeping them so that they can be inspected.
d) It refers to the solid pine settees.

*Letter 7.4*

a) By the use of 'at last'.
b) It refers to the fact that the goods were damaged.

*Drills*

1)
a) Although the packets were intact on arrival, I discovered that the digital scales were damaged.
b) Although the boxes were intact when we received them, I discovered that the infra-red sunray lamps were spoilt.
c) Although the cases were intact at the depot, our agent discovered that the armchairs were broken.
d) Although the cardboard boxes were intact at the office, my assistant discovered that the telephone tables were below standard.

2)
a) We acknowledge reception of the cooking ranges which you sent to us according to our order of the 1st instant.
b) I acknowledge reception of the 'Permo Focus' binoculars which you sent to us according to our order of the 24th instant.
c) Mr Wigzell acknowledges reception of the indoor aerials which you sent to us according to our order of the 3rd instant.
d) Our client acknowledges reception of the 'Shorty' boots with elastic sides which you sent to us according to our order of the 8th instant.

3)
a) I regret to inform you that our shipment of mini-ovens was delivered to us this morning in a very bad state.
b) The Manager regrets to inform you that our consignment of spring mattresses was delivered to us yesterday in a very bad state.
c) I regret to inform you that our boxes of pyjamas were delivered to us on the 5th

August in a very bad state.
d) We regret to inform you that our packet of shirts was delivered to us this afternoon in a very bad state.

*Exercise 7.1*

Dear Sir, We have just taken delivery of the articles in our order No. 313/2. Although the consignment was intact when we unpacked it, we regret to have to inform you that some of the sheds were broken. You can understand our disappointment. We have told the shipper about the damage and kept boxes and contents so that they may be inspected. Yours faithfully, Jessie Carter, Manageress.

*Exercise 7.2*

Dear Sirs, Your shipment was at last delivered yesterday at the freight station in Carlisle. We regret to inform you that the goods did not come up to their usual standard. We have told the shipper about the damage and kept the boxes and their contents so that they may be inspected. Yours faithfully, Rachel Chan.

*Exercise 7.3*

Dear Sirs, We acknowledge reception of the canned fish and meat which you sent to us according to our order of the 5th instant. Unfortunately, I regret to have to inform you that the goods were clearly damaged. We are now returning the damaged items and would be grateful if you would replace them immediately. Yours faithfully, Jacques Duhaut, Managing Director.

## UNIT 8 - Apologies and replies to complaints

*Letter 8.1*

a) He asked his Shipping Department.
b) Because the goods were damaged by a storm.
c) He is going to send off the order as soon as possible.
d) It refers to the wine glasses.

*Letter 8.2*

a) Because he can't find a record of the order.
b) He wants her to send the number and the date of the order.
c) By assuring her that he will give the matter priority.

*Letter 8.3*

a) Because her client has been overcharged.
b) Because they are changing computers.

*Letter 8.4*

a) They became unfastened during transport.
b) It was the fault of a new packer.
c) He has replaced the articles.
d) It refers to the wooden spring bed frames.

*Drills*

1)
a) In reply to your letter of 9th February on the subject of the non-delivery of the circular

saws, I have asked our manager who informs me that the cardboard boxes were sent yesterday.

b) In reply to your letter of 23rd June on the subject of the non-delivery of the curtains we have asked our foreman who informs us that the packets were shipped yesterday afternoon.

c) In reply to your letter of 5th August on the subject of the non-delivery of the slide projectors, my assistant assistant has asked our Shipping Agent who informs him that the containers were dispatched last week.

d) In reply to your letter of 8th July on the subject of the non-delivery of the brushed wool jogging suits, we have asked our representative who informs us that the bales were sent this morning.

2)
a) The Sales Manager very much regrets that, until now, he has been unable to send you the high-precision astronomical telescopes that you ordered.

b) We very much regret that, until now, we have been unable to dispatch 6/12 V battery chargers you ordered.

c) My colleague very much regrets that, until now, he has been unable to ship the 50 tool kits you ordered.

d) I very much regret that, until now, I have been unable to send the car loudspeakers you ordered.

3)
a) I was very put to hear that the 12 V car vacuum cleaners I dispatched by rail were damaged during transport.

b) Mr. Laurence was very put out to hear that the electric paint sprays he shipped by sea were scratched during transport.

c) I was very put out to hear that the pleated trousers I sent by post were spoilt during transport.

d) We were very put out to hear that the antique hallstand we dispatched by road was broken during transport.

*Exercise 8.1*

Dear Sir, In reply to your letter of the 1st April on the subject of the non-delivery of the 10 filing cabinets, we have asked our Shipping Department and they inform us that the goods were damaged by a fire that we had in our warehouse last week. As soon as things are back to normal, we hope to be able to continue as usual. Please excuse us for all the inconvenience that this may have caused you. Yours faithfully, Derek Blackstone, Manager.

*Exercise 8.2*

Dear Sir, We very much regret that, until now, we have not been able to send you the settees you ordered. You can rest assured that we shall make sure that this order will be dealt with as soon as possible. Please excuse us for all the inconvenience that this may have caused you. Yours faithfully, Oliver Gardner, Export Manager.

*Exercise 8.3*

Dear Sir, We have received your letter of 9th September and very much regret that, until now, we have not been able to send you your order. We are in the process of changing computers, which has led to a certain amount of duplication of invoices. Please excuse us for all the inconvenience that this may have caused you. Yours faithfully, Gerald Arkwright, Sales Manager.

## UNIT 9 - Complaints and replies about payment

*Letter 9.1*

a) He hasn't received payment for the last two shipments.
b) He suggests that it was caused by an oversight in the accounts department.

*Letter 9.2*

a) The fact that they have not settled their bill.
b) Payment of the bill and an excuse for the delay.

*Letter 9.3*

a) To inform the client that payment was due.
b) He's trying to overcome the problem by sending an instalment.

*Letter 9.4*

a) It suggests that they have always paid on time in the past.
b) Because of hurricane damage.

*Drills*

1)
a) I would like to draw your attention to my statement of account of 8 August.
b) The manager would like to draw your attention to his cheque of 20 January.
c) We would like to draw your attention to our receipt of 4 March.
d) I would like to draw your attention to my advertisement of 18 October.

2)
a) The damage caused by the rain resulted in serious delays and I would be very grateful if you would allow me a fortnight extra.
b) The delay caused by the strike resulted in serious shortages and the staff would be grateful if you would allow them a week extra.
c) The hold-up caused by the cold weather resulted in serious problems and the manager would be grateful if you would allow him a month extra.
d) The stoppage caused by the the flood resulted in serious hold-ups and we would be grateful if you would allow us a few days extra.

3)
a) I wish to remind you that your account No. A-23-13 dated 9 January, has not yet been settled.
b) The manager wishes to remind you that your bills Nos. 325-X32-1 & 2 dated 11 February have not yet been settled.
c) Our Accounts Department wishes to remind you that your account No. B43-430-1 dated 23 March has not yet been settled.
d) Mr. Springfield wishes to remind you that your bills Nos. X432-76 & 7 dated 14 December have not yet been settled.

*Exercise 9.1*

Dear Sirs, We would like to draw your attention to our bill of 12th February. As we have not yet received your settlement of last February, we would like you to give this situation your utmost attention. If you have already transferred the amount in question, please take no notice of this request. I am sure that this delay is due to an oversight in your accounts department and while awaiting settlement, we remain, Yours faithfully, George Hicks, Accounts Department.

*Exercise 9.2*

Dear Sir, We wish to remind you that your invoice No. 896/1A dated 8th August has not yet been settled and we would be very happy if you would send payment as soon as possible. We are very grateful for your understanding in this matter. Yours faithfully, Eric Jones, Customer Accounts.

*Exercise 9.3*

Dear Sirs, I have certainly received your letter of 8th January concerning the non-settlement of our order A/97867. As we are experiencing temporary cash-flow problems, we are sending you half of the amount as an instalment and we shall pay the remainder over the next three months. Thanking you in advance, I remain, Yours faithfully, J. Bressler.

## UNIT 10 - Status enquiries

*Letter 10.1*

a) Because he has received a large order from a client wanting to open a credit account.
b) He has enclosed the client's name and address on a separate slip of paper.
c) He wants to know whether it is safe to allow the client goods to the value of DM 50 000.

*Letter 10.2*

a) Carlton Incorporated wants to open an account with Milton Jackson's company.
b) He wants to know whether it is wise to do business with them on a credit basis.
c) He has enclosed an international reply coupon.

*Letter 10.3*

a) She wants information about the quality of their work and their after sales service.

*Letter 10.4*

a) They have placed a large order for household goods.
b) They will be required to pay every three months.

*Drills*

1)
a) The Director has just received an important order from the business we spoke about.
b) I have just received an important order from the corporation you mentioned.
c) We have just received an important order from the organization I mentioned on the 'phone yesterday.
d) My partner has just received an important order from the agency he mentioned last week.

2)
a) I would particularly like to know if this business enjoys a sound financial situation and if I can let them have machinery up to a credit limit of 100,000 FF.
b) Mr. Laurence would particularly like to know if this business enjoys a sound financial situation and if he can let them have merchandise up to a credit limit of $50,000.

c) We would particularly like to know if this business enjoys a sound financial situation and if we can let them have soft furnishings up to a credit limit of 2,000,000 pesetas.
d) We would particularly like to know if this business enjoys a sound financial situation and if we can let them have machine tools up to a credit limit of £50,000.

3)
a) Before finally committing myself, I would be obliged if you would give me your opinion on their financial standing.
b) Before finally committing herself, Mrs. Jackson would be obliged if you would give her your opinion on their ability to deliver on time.
c) Before finally committing themselves, the partners would be obliged if you would give them your opinion on their ability to fulfil orders quickly.
d) Before finally committing ourselves, we would be obliged if you would give us your opinion on their sales network.

*Exercise 10.1*

Dear Sir, We have just received an important order from the company whose name you will find on the enclosed slip. Could you please let us have full information on this company's financial position? We know that you often have business dealings with them so we thought that you, better than anyone else, could give us information about their financial situation. Do you think that we could safely do business with them? Needless to say all information will remain confidential. Yours faithfully, Charles Macintosh, Manager.

*Exercise 10.2*

Dear Sir, We would be very grateful if we could obtain information about Calton Incorporated of Seattle, Washington, USA, who would like to open an account and who have given us your name as a reference. We would particularly like to know if this company enjoys a sound financial situation and if we can let them have goods up to a credit limit of DM 50,000. In the hope of a speedy reply, we enclose an international reply coupon. Yours faithfully, Karl Rauch.

*Exercise 10.3*

Dear Sirs, We would be very grateful if we could obtain information about Bayart Père Fils & Cie, who would like to open an account and who have given us your name as a reference. Although we are sure of their ability to pay, we would like **confirmation\*** that their financial situation guarantees quarterly payments of up to 6,000,000 FF. You can rest assured that this information will be kept strictly confidential. John Walsh, Manager,

## UNIT 11 - *Cancellations and alterations*

*Letter 11.1*

a) By claiming that the error accidentally "slipped" into the order.
b) He ordered the wrong goods.

*Letter 11.2*

a) He's been waiting for it for almost a month.
b) He has realised that he has enough equalizers in stock.

*Letter 11.3*

a)  It informed him that the company could not fulfil his order.
b)  Because he must have the goods by a certain date.

Letter 11.4

a)  Because the supplier has not got the goods in stock.
b)  A revised order.

*Drills*

1)
a)  I am obliged to inform you that a mistake has slipped into my order No. B-4325 of 8th January last. Instead of: Jackets 100% cotton, it should read: Jackets 100% brushed cotton.
b)  Our customer is obliged to inform you that a mistake has slipped into his order No. A-34/23-1 of 12th October last. Instead of: stereo headphones, it should read: mini-stereo headphones.
c)  Our customers are obliged to inform you that a mistake has slipped into their order No. X-435 of 15th March last. Instead of: 'Charlotte' dolls, it should read: 'Laurie' dolls.
d)  We are obliged to inform you that a mistake has slipped into our order No. 4532-1 of 17th February last. Instead of: Batch of 10 video cassettes 2 x 120 mn Ref: 132.12, it should read: Batch of 12 video cassettes 2 x 140 mn Ref: 132.10.

2)
a)  On 9th July my assistant ordered 5 shower curtains 80 x 150 cm. which should be delivered this week.
b)  On 8th August I ordered 10 leather office armchairs which should be delivered at the end of the week.
c)  On 18th June our customers ordered 100 Grandfather, cotton night-shirts which should be delivered today.
d)  On 10th November we ordered 20 pocket electronic chess games which should be delivered in a few days.

3)
a)  As your shop has not got these articles in stock I would be obliged if you would cancel my order for 10 GEC black and white portable TV sets and replace them with 10 GEC portable colour TV sets.
b)  As they have not got these articles in stock, the manageress would be obliged they would cancel her order for 6 electric toasters and replace them with 6 electric mini ovens.
c)  As the warehouse has not got these articles in stock, our clients would be obliged if you would cancel their order for 25 articulated desk-top lamps, black and replace them with 10 black and 15 red.
d)  As you have not got these articles in stock, we would be obliged if you would cancel our order for "après-ski" boots in three colours and replace them with blue "après-ski" boots with laces.

*Exercise 11.1*

Dear Madam, As you have not got these articles in stock, we would be obliged if you would cancel our order No. 73891/43A. I hope that, in view of our long-standing dealings with you, you will accept this change. We look forward to receiving a favourable reply,

Yours faithfully, Margaret Heath, Manageress.

*Exercise 11.2*

Dear Sir, We are sorry to learn from your letter of 9th October that it is impossible for you to fulfil our order No. 875-326 according to the stipulated details. As you have not got these articles in stock, we would be obliged if you would cancel our order for 6 cases of double sided, double density 3½" micro floppy disks and replace it with 6 cases of DS, DD 5¼" floppy disks. Please find enclosed a revised order form. Yours faithfully, Max Kaminsky, Overseas Sales.

*Exercise 11.3*

Dear Sir, We am obliged to inform you that a mistake has slipped into our order No. A/147B of 5th October last. Instead of: 200 FR/6736A transistors, it should read: 200 F6836B transistors. We should be obliged if you would confirm as soon as possible that this change is acceptable. Yours faithfully, Gerald Booth, Manager.

UNIT 12 - *Introducing a new salesperson*

*Letter 12.1*

a) He is the new Burnley Plastics representative.
b) He's taking a full set of samples.

*Letter 12.2*

a) He heard that the company was interested in their products and his representative was about to visit the area.
b) To arrange a visit by the representative.

*Letter 12.3*

a) He's going to make his visit sometime during the coming week.
b) Bill will contact him personally.

*Letter 12.4*

a) He is the new area representative.
b) He's trying to pormote the Nylon models.

*Drills*

1)
a) My commercial traveller in your area, John Harrington, will call to see you shortly.
b) Our representative in your area, Marie Russell, will call to see you soon.
c) My colleagues in your area, Philip Roberts and Oscar Peters, will call to see you at the beginning of next week.

2)
a) I have pleasure in announcing the visit of my representative, Madelaine Godart, to Paris with a complete set of samples of our new range. She will call on you in a few days' time.
b) Mr Jackson has pleasure in announcing the visit of his assistant, Peter Philips, to Cologne with a complete set of our brochures. He will call on you shortly.
c) We have pleasure in announcing the visit of our new colleague, Edward Anderson,

to Vienna with a complete set of our latest products. He will call on you at the beginning of the week.

3)
a)  We are happy to inform you that our commercial traveller, Charles Sarvan, will be in your area during the the week with a complete assortment of our padded jackets as well as our multi-coloured jogging suits.
b)  Mrs Saville is happy to inform you that her assistant, Isabel Pierce, will soon be in your area with a complete assortment of our multi-purpose cardboard filing boxes as well as our pull-out plastic filing systems.
c)  We are happy to inform you that our partner, Michael Clarke, will be in your area next week with a complete assortment of our range of non-stick kitchenware as well as our cutlery.

*Exercise 12.1*

Dear Madam, We learn with great pleasure that you are interested in our type of merchandise. We are happy to inform you that our representative, Mark Blackwell, will very shortly be in your area with a complete assortment of our latest products as well as our current range. I am sure that you will find Mr Blackwell both pleasant and obliging, and that you will appreciate his professional qualities. Yours faithfully, Greg Thomson.

*Exercise 12.2*

Dear Sirs, We have pleasure in announcing the visit of our new representative, Hussain Dhaif, to Bahrain with a complete set of our new samples. He will call on you in the course of next week. We would be grateful if you would let us know as soon as possible whether a visit is convenient so that we can arrange a meeting. We hope that this arrangement suits you. Yours faithfully, Carl Linderman.

*Exercise 12.3*

Dear Sirs, Our new representative in your area, Michel Gaillard, will call to see you in the course of the coming week. He will show you, on our behalf, a collection of our latest models. We would particularly like to draw your attention to the exceptional quality of the models in stainless steel which sell at extremely competitive prices. We hope that you will favour us with an order which, it goes without saying, will be processed with the utmost care. Yours faithfully, Hans Hassler, Director.

## UNIT 13 - *Insurance*

*Letter 13.1*

a)  Because the proposal form was attached.
b)  Because the policy is not ready yet.

*Letter 13.2*

a)  He wants him to get the damage assessed by his own expert and settle the claim.
b)  The customs report.

*Letter 13.3*

a)  The assessor's report and a letter from the shipping agent.
b)  He wants him to replace the damaged goods.

*Exercise 13*

Dear Sirs, Flight DA 765 landed on time at Gatwick airport this morning as expected, but when our agent inspected the cargo, he noticed that one of the boxes in container No. 12 had been damaged. We contacted our insurance representative in Brighton and he agreed to be present when the box was opened. On inspection, he found that several of the articles were spoilt. We are sending you his report and, as you are the policy holder, we would be obliged if you could make the necessary application to the insurance underwriters to claim for compensation. Needless to say, because of this mishap, we are in a very embarrassing situation as regards our customers. We would, therefore, be very grateful if you would send us replacements by air freight as soon as possible. Yours faithfully,

## UNIT 14 - *Appointing agents*

*Letter 14.1*

a)  Probably by sending their own sales representative.
b)  He tries to make it attractive by offering a commission of 15% on net sales.

*Letter 14.2*

a)  He wants a sole agency to avoid competition from another agent.
b)  One of the problems is that customers prefer fresh foods.

*Exercise 14*

Dear Sirs, The excellent quality of your agricultural productss, a selection of which we recently saw in action in France, impressed us very much. We have since seen your latest catalogue and are interested to know whether you have considered appointing an agent in the UK. As a leading firm of importers and distributors of many years' standing, we have an extensive sales organization and a very wide knowledge of the UK market. We think your products would sell very well here, and are prepared to enter into a business relationship with you. We are also interested in handling a sole agency for you, which we think would be to our mutual advantage. Please let us know if you are interested in these proposals. Yours faithfully.

## UNIT 15 - *Overseas payments*

*Letter 15.1*

a)  He wants him to pay by a letter of credit.
b)  They will process the order when they receive the letter of credit.

*Letter 15.2*

a)  He was informed by his agent.
b)  They'll be shipped as soon as the credit has been confirmed by his bank.

*Letter 15.3*

a)  He'll be sending it to Barclays Bank in Guernsey.
b)  He'll send a draft.

*Exercise 15*

Dear Sir, We acknowledge with thanks the receipt of your order which we note was sent on 15 January. Our representative, Mr Blunt, informs us that the goods are being prepared for shipment. We note that you will arrange payment by Irrevocable Letter of Credit in our favour, to be valid until 1 March. As soon as we receive notification that the credit has been opened, the goods will be packed and shipped in accordance with your instructions. Please be assured that all your orders will have our most careful attention and we look forward to further co-operation with you in the future, Yours faithfully,

## UNIT 16 - Job applications

*Letter 16.1*

a) Because she wants to apply for the post of bilingual secretary with AGCOM Ltd.
b) She has introduced a new filing system and has completely modernized the office routine.

*Letter 16.2*

a) He was the private secretary to the owner of James Young plc.
b) He wants Mr Trulle to give him an interview.

*Letter 16.3*

a) She worked as a proof-reader for an advertising company.
b) She studied at the University of Kent and the Alliance Française. She also studied for a year in Grenoble.

*Exercise 16*

Dear Sirs, In reply to your advertisement in *The Guardian* I should be grateful if you would consider my application for this post. I have been working as an audio-typist for more than six years; my speed in shorthand is 110 words a minute and in typing, 60 words a minute. I have recently updated my qualifications by taking a course in computer studies. I am now very proficient in word processing (WordStar 5.5) and familiar with data bases such as D.Base 3. I am experienced in all kinds of office work and have a good knowledge of up-to-date accountancy programs. I am 26 and have a clean driving licence. I enclose my curriculum vitae and copies of three testimonials. I very much hope that you will give me the opportunity of attending an interview. Yours faithfully,

## UNIT 17 - Dealing with job applications

*Letter 17.1*

a) He wants her to attend for interview on the following Wednesday, the 13 March at 2.30 p.m.
b) He wants her to contact his secretary for a new date and time.

*Letter 17.2*

a) She wants him to sign two copies of the contract of employment and return them to her office.
b) He would contact her if he wanted to know more about the contract.

*Letter 17.3*

a) It took him a week.
b) By saying that he will keep his application on file.

*Exercise 17*

Dear Miss Foxwell, Thank you for your letter of 10 January applying for the post of bilingual secretary. I should like to take your application a stage further and would be glad if you could come here for an interview on Friday next, 26 January, at 2.30p.m. If that day or time is not suitable, will you kindly let me know, preferably by telephone, and I will try to arrange the interview for a time and a day more convenient to you. I look forward to hearing from you and meeting you in person on Friday. Yours sincerely, John Pattison, Recruitment.

## UNIT 18 - Personal references

*Letter 18.1*

a) He is applying for the post of Sales Representative.
b) Because he is familiar with his work at Llama Gabilondo y Cia, S.A.

*Letter 18.2*

a) Because he encouraged her to continue her study of German and helped her prepare for her final examinations.
b) She wants him to send it to the personnel manager of Trans-World.

*Letter 18.3*

a) He wants the information to be kept confidential.
b) She became secretary to the Overseas Sales Manager.

*Exercise 18*

Dear Sirs, Miss Jackson joined our staff as a trainee secretary five years ago. She has continuously tried to improve her professional ability, taking evening courses in secretarial practice, Italian and electronic communications. A year ago, she became the personal assistant to the Sales Manager. Part of her work now is to handle all overseas correspondence. She is also responsible for arranging sales promotion meetings, and preparing reports and minutes. We feel very confident that she would be a highly suitable person for the post of personal assistant to the Export Manager of your company and we offer our wholehearted recommendation. Yours faithfully,

## UNIT 19 - Sales letters

*Letter 19.1*

a) It refers to sales literature, samples and a display kit.
b) He gives full details on prices, discounts, incentives and marketing materials.

*Letter 19.2*

a) They have 10 cooking speeds, touch-sensitive controls, an automatically cleaned base and a special browning adapter.
b) By saying that they come from high-grade manufacturers with reliable quality control.

*Letter 19.3*

a) He was well-known for his tradition of quality service.
b) He is the owner of Dover Travel.

*Exercise 19*

Dear Sirs, We have great pleasure in informing you that we have just opened an agency for high-pressure cleaning pumps and our connection with the main manufacturers allows us to supply our goods at competitive prices. In addition, our Hamburg office is organized to locate and supply very quickly products that are not available on the German market. Please do not hesitate to send us a trial order by using the order form in the brochure. We are offering a reduction of 15% on all orders received before the end of the year. Yours faithfully,

## UNIT 20 - Hotel reservations

*Letter 20.1*

a) He will be staying for three nights.
b) He would like his room at the back.

*Letter 20.2*

a) He requires a small suite and access to a conference room, plus a single room for his secretary.
b) She wants confirmation of the dates and details of charges.

*Letter 20.3*

a) A single room with a bath.
b) He can get from the airport by the Airport Shuttle Service.

*Exercise 20*

Dear Sirs, Myself and five members of our staff will be coming to London on business for 1st March to 6th April. We would like to book two single rooms and two double rooms with showers for six nights. We shall require breakfast in our rooms but will take dinner in the main dining room in the evenings. I would greatly appreciate it if you could let me have the same room at the back of the hotel as I had last year because the rooms overlooking the street are rather noisy. Our group will arrive at Heathrow at about 11 a.m., but as we have be meetings until the early evening, we shall probably check in just in time for dinner at about 7 p.m. I look forward to an early confirmation so that I can complete the arrangements for the visit. Yours faithfully,

# APPENDIX
## LAYOUT – THE PARTS OF AN ENGLISH BUSINESS LETTER

# SOUTHWAY BUILDING SOCIETY

*Head Office:* [1]
30/32 Friars Walk,
Polegate, East Sussex BN7 2LW
Telephone: (0265) 476586
Telefax: (0265) 476598
Telex: 897564 (SBS G)

*Managing Director - P. Ketteridge FCDSI*

Mr J. G. Howard, [3]
St Margaret's Crescent,
Harrogate,
Yorkshire YU8 7JK                    5 October 1990 [2]
UK

Your ref:  LM/GH [4]
Our ref:  DMkj/CG

Dear Mr Howard, [5]

Re: Mortgage Account No. 1876435 - 17 Roman Road [6]

[7]

Thank you for your letter of 29 September, and I note
that you would like details of cover to the sum of
£80,000 on the buildings at 17 Roman Road.

I enclose herewith a booklet detailing the premium
rates for standard cover and for cover to include
accidental damage.

Please contact me as soon as possible to advise:

1. Whether cover is still required.
2. Type of cover required.

I shall then put the necessary arrangements in hand.

Yours sincerely, [8]

[9]

K. J. Horner,
Manager - Insurance Services [10]

1 The name, address, telephone number etc., of the company from where the letter is written.
2 The date.
3 The name and address of the company to which the letter is being sent; sometimes called the "inside address".
4 Reference letters and/or numbers.
5 The salutation.
6 The subject line.
7 The body of the letter.
8 The complimentary close.
9 The signature and name of the person writing the letter.
10 The title and position of the person signing the letter.

# *Notes*

1) The address of the sender is written on the right-hand side of the page at the beginning of the letter. Of course, many companies have theirs printed in the centre or to one side. The number of the house is written first, followed by the name of the road or street, e.g.

| | |
|---|---|
| Number of the road (Rd.): | **12 Watling Rd.,** |
| or street (St.): | **12 Meadow St.,** |
| or avenue (Ave.): | **12 Upperton Ave.,** |

Other abbreviations are:

| | | | |
|---|---|---|---|
| **Sq.** | Square | **Cres.** | Crescent |
| **Terr.** | Terrace | **Pl.** | Place |
| **Ct.** | Court | **Gdns.** | Gardens |

The following cannot be abbreviated:

| | | |
|---|---|---|
| **Close** | **Drive** | **Grove** |
| **Lane** | **Mews** | **Way** |

This is followed by the name of the town and the county. If the city is large and well known, such as Leeds or Birmingham, it is not necessary to write the name of the county. The town or county is followed by the postcode, which has no full stop after it. If you are writing from abroad, **England** or **UK** must be on a separate line, e.g.

| | |
|---|---|
| Name | **Mr H. James,** |
| Road | **16 Terminus Road,** |
| Town | **Eastbourne,** |
| County | **East Sussex,** |
| Postcode | **BN21 2PY** |
| Country | **UK** |

Each line is followed by a comma, except for the post code and the country, if mentioned. Some companies, however, omit commas.

2) The date is normally written under the address, but this is not always so on printed letterheads.

There are several ways of writing the date.

> **5 October 1990**
> **5th October, 1990**
> **5th Oct., 1990**
> **October 5th, 1990**
> **Oct. 5th, 1990**
> **5/10/87** or **5.10.87** (day, month, year)

In the USA the month is written first, then the day, then the year, e.g. **5 October 1990** would be written **10/5/90**.

Never write **of** in the date ("5th of October").

3) Below the address, but on the left-hand side of the page, you should write the name and address of the person and company you are writing to, the inside address. If you do not know his or her name, use his or her title, e.g. **The Manager, The Director**:

> **The Manager,**
> **Personal Service Business Systems,**
> **32 King St.,**
> **Birmingham BM1 7UJ**

4) The reference is usually typed on the same line as the date, but on the left. It usually consists of the initials of the typist and of the person who signs the letter. Sometimes other letters and figures are used, so that the letter can be easily filed.

5    a) If you do not know the name of the person you are writing to, the salutation will be:

> **Dear Sir** (to a man) or **Dear Sirs**
> **Dear Madam** (to a woman).

b) If you are writing to someone you know, or someone whose name you know, or someone who has written to you first, begin:

> **Dear Mr Smith**
> **Dear Mrs Smith** (a married woman)
> **Dear Miss Smith** (an unmarried woman)
> **Dear Ms Smith** (a woman, either married or unmarried)

or with professional titles:

**Dear Dr Smith**
**Dear Professor Smith**

c) If you are writing to a company you can put **Messrs** before the name of the company if it contains one or more personal names:

**Messrs Peter Greenfield and Co. Ltd,**
**Messrs Jackson and Potter plc** (= public limited company)
**Messrs Philpot & Sons**
**Messrs Gorringe Bros** (= Brothers)

d) If the company does not contain a personal name, **The** is usually written before it:

**The Southern Electric Co. Ltd**
**The Intervac Travel Association**

e) If you are writing to a person who has a particular position, write **The** before the position:

**The Director of Studies.**
**The Manager**
**The Sales Manager**

f) If you are writing to people of other nationalities, use the style of the country, if you know it:

**Herr Rauch**
**Sr. Gonzales**
**M. Godart**

6) The subject matter of the letter is often indicated in the subject line, which is written below the salutation. Sometimes **Re:** (with reference to) is used to introduce the subject of the letter. If not, then reference to the date in the first line of an answer is enough to make known what the subject is, e.g.

**Thank you for your letter of 18th January**

7) There are two main styles for the body of the letter: **blocked** and **indented**. In the blocked style, each line begins at the left hand margin. There is no punctuation before the salutation; punctuation only occurs in the body of the letter itself. The letter on page 146 uses the block style.

The indented style blocks the inside address etc., places the date on the right and indents each paragraph of the body of the letter. Punctuation is used throughout the letter, e.g.

```
The Manager,
Forest Holdings plc,
Crawley,
Sussex HJ3 45K
U.K.                              17th January 19..


Dear Sir,

    We thank you for your letter of 15th January
in which you outlined your plans for the
future development of the company.

    I have consulted my partners and they agree
that we should meet at the earliest opportunity.

    My secretary will be in touch with you very
shortly to arrange a convenient date and time.

                    Yours faithfully,



                    Sidney George,
                    Senior Partner
```

Most companies have rules regarding which style should be used. In practice the rules are not strictly adhered to and a mixture of both styles is often the result.

8) The complimentary close has two simple rules:

a) If you begin your letter, **Dear Sir or Madam** that is, if you are writing to a stranger then you must end, **Yours faithfully**.
b) If you are writing to someone whose name you know, or someone who has written to you first, you end with, **Yours sincerely**.

9) & 10) The signature is followed by the name of the person signing the letter followed by their title.

If the person who has dictated the letter is not present to sign it, the typist or some other person will sign it instead. In this case, it is usual practice to write the letters **p.p.** or **per pro** – (**per procurationem** = on behalf of) – before the name of the person signing the letter.

Other additions to the bottom of a letter might be:

> **Encl:** or **Encs:** Enclosures
> **Copy to** or **Copies to**

**Private and Confidential** is written under the inside address when the letter deals with such subjects as loans, trade references, etc.

**For the attention of...** can also placed under the inside address.

*Addressing an envelope*

The address on an envelope takes the same form as the inside address in the letter except that the name of the town and the country are often written in capitals. The postal code is written in capitals and should be the last line with a space after the line above. This is because the bottom line is recorded mechanically at the sorting office.

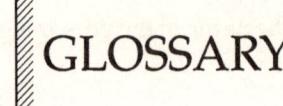

# GLOSSARY

*The number in brackets refers to the unit in which the word is first used.*

## A

| | |
|---|---|
| **accepted** (5) | usual, allowed |
| **access** (20) | way in |
| **accommodation** (20) | place to live |
| **accompanying** (4) | sent at the same time, included |
| **acknowledge** (1) | to say that you have received something |
| **acquisition** (19) | buying |
| **adapter** (19) | apparatus joining one piece of electrical equipment to another |
| **adequate** (19) | enough for the purpose |
| **adhere to** (11) | to be faithful to |
| **appoint** (14) | to choose for a position |
| **appointment** (16) | agreement to meet at a certain time and place |
| **appreciate** (5) | to understand and enjoy the good qualities of something |
| **appropriately** (3) | in a suitable way |
| **assessor** (13) | someone who decides on the value of something |
| **assortment** (12) | various examples |
| **attachment** (3) | something that is fixed to something else. |
| **available** (19) | able to be obtained, on sale |

## B

| | |
|---|---|
| **bale** (5) | large package usually of soft material |
| **batch** (6) | number of items grouped together |
| **bilingual** (16) | able to speak two languages |
| **bulk** (2) | in large quantities |

## C

| | |
|---|---|
| **capabilities** (17) | the things you are able to do |
| **cash flow** (9) | the money coming into a business |
| **catering** (2) | providing and serving food and drinks |
| **challenge** (16) | something which requires action, interest or thought |
| **chandelier** (6) | large glass holder for electric lights |
| **circular** (1) | printed advertisement or notice given to a large number of people |
| **circular** (3) | round |
| **claim** (13) | demand |
| **collapsible** (3) | can be folded for easy storing |
| **commit oneself** (10) | to promise to do something |
| **competitive** (12) | trying to be better than others |

| | |
|---|---|
| compensation (13) | payment for a loss |
| competence (16) | ability to do what is needed |
| concerning (5) | about, with regard to |
| confirm (20) | to make certain, give proof of |
| confidential (18) | secret |
| considerable (14) | quite large |
| confirm (4) | to give proof of |
| consequently (8) | as a result |
| consignment (6) | a number of goods sent together |
| convenient (12) | suitable |
| correspond (6) | match |
| cot (5) | small bed for a baby |
| counter (19) | narrow table in a shop for serving people |
| cover note (13) | letter saying that you are insured against loss |
| credit, letter of (15) | letter from a customer promising to pay by a certain date |
| credit note (8) | note instead of money |
| crush (8) | to press flat |
| current (1) | now, at the moment |
| C.V. (curriculum vitae) (16) | written details of one's education and past work experience |

## D

| | |
|---|---|
| deal with (8) | to take action about |
| deliberation (17) | thought, consideration |
| disappointment (7) | sadness because what was expected did not take place |
| discount (19) | a reduction in price |
| discover (11) | to find something for the first time |
| dispatch (8) | to send, ship |
| display (19) | to show goods in a shop |
| distributor (1) | dealer |
| draft (15) | a cheque issued by a bank, an order to pay |
| draft plans (1) | the first written form or plan of something |
| dresser (6) | a piece of furniture for holding cups and plates |
| duplicate (5) | two |
| duplication (8) | copying |

## E

| | |
|---|---|
| edible (5) | able to be eaten |
| efficiently (19) | well, so as to produce the desired effect |
| embarrassing (13 | making one feel ashamed |
| encouragement (18) | hope and confidence given to someone |
| enquiry (inquiry) (8) | asking questions about something |
| estimate (13) | to calculate (approximately) the amount of something |
| evaluate (13) | to calculate the value of something |
| executive (16) | a person who carries out decisions in business |
| excursion (16) | a short journey made for pleasure |
| expectation (16) | hope |

**expedite** (3)     to send a shipment as quickly as possible
**explore** (14)     to examine carefully
**extractor** (5)     a fan for sending smelly air out of a kitchen

F

**favour** (12)     to act kindly
**favourable** (11)     saying what one wants to hear
**featuring** (19)     included or shown
**field** (16)     area
**filing** (16)     system for classifying and storing documents
**fluent** (16)     speaking and writing a language smoothly and with ease
**foreman** (8)     a worker in charge of other workers
**fortnight** (9)     two weeks
**fragile** (5)     easily broken or damages
**frame** (8)     a wooden border, as around a picture
**fulfil** (11)     to cause to happen
**fund** (17)     a sum of money reserved for a special purpose
**further** (1)     more

G

**gaining** (16)     obtaining, getting
**gasket** (3)     a piece of material placed between two surfaces so that oil or gas cannot escape
**goose** (3)     a large white bird which looks like a duck
**graduate** (16)     person who has completed a university degree course
**grateful** (3)     thankful

H

**herewith** (3)     with this letter
**hesitate** (17)     to pause or wait before an action
**hinge** (6)     a metal joint on a door
**hold-up** (9)     a delay
**hood** (5)     a cover over a cooking stove
**hurricane** (9)     a storm with a very strong wind

I

**identical** (6)     exactly the same
**incentive** (19)     something which encourages you to greater activity
**inconvenience** (8)     a state of difficulty when things do not go well
**incident** (11)     an event, something that happens
**inclusive** (20)     including all the dates
**insist** (11)     to order something to happen
**instalment** (9)     a single payment, part of many payments
**instant** (3)     happening now, e.g. this month
**intact** (7)     not spoilt or damaged
**invoice** (5)     a bill for goods received

**issue** (15)                something (especially printed) given out

## J

**jack** (1)                a tool for lifting a car off the ground

## K

**kit** (19)                a set of things, especially tools

## L

**ladder** (3)                steps used for climbing
**Lading, Bill of** (15)                a document acknowledging receipt of goods for shipping
**laminate** (4)                strong material made by joining many thin sheets together
**launching** (1)                putting on the market
**leaflet** (1)                a small sheet of printed information
**locate** (8)                to find
**loft** (5)                a room in a roof
**long-standing** (11)                something which has existed for a long time

## M

**maintain** (19)                to continue to do or have as before
**maritime** (7)                concerning the sea and ships
**mobile** (5)                a hanging decoration
**mulching** (4)                improving the soil by covering it
**mutually** (14)                equally

## N

**net** (14)                the price after all expenses have been paid

## O

**opportunity** (16)                chance
**outfit** (6)                the clothes needed for a particular job or sport
**outing** (17)                a short pleasure trip
**outline** (2)                the main ideas
**outstanding** (2)                not yet paid
**over** (9)                during
**overalls** (4)                clothes worn by workers over other clothes
**overcharge** (8)                to ask for too much money for something
**overrun** (9)                to continue beyond a time limit
**overseas** (1)                abroad
**oversight** (9)                a failure to notice or do something

## P

**particularly** (1)                especially, very much
**pine** (7)                the white or yellowish wood of the pine tree
**pleat** (8)                a narrow fold in cloth

| | |
|---|---|
| **polo-necked** (4) | roll-necked |
| **precision** (8) | exactness |
| **preliminary** (2) | coming before, first |
| **premises** (19) | building, especially one occupied by a business |
| **preserves** (14) | jam |
| **processed** (15) | prepared, dealt with |
| **professional** (12) | well trained in his job |
| **profitable** (14) | likely to produce a profit |
| **pro forma invoice** (1) | invoice which tells the customer the price of the goods before they are sent |
| **proof-reader** (16) | someone who checks a written text for mistakes |
| **profound** (8) | very deep, serious |
| **proposal** (2) | suggestion |
| **proposal form** (13) | form to be completed in order to obtain insurance |
| **proprietor** (19) | owner |
| **put out** (8) | unhappy, hurt |

## Q

| | |
|---|---|
| **qualification** (16) | a certificate or other proof of study |
| **quarterly** (10) | every three months |
| **quilt** (3) | a thick cover for a bed |
| **quotation** (2) | suggested price |

## R

| | |
|---|---|
| **rack** (3) | a frame with bars and hooks for holding things |
| **realize** (14) | to understand and believe |
| **reclined** (3) | lying down |
| **recommendation** (14) | advice, praise |
| **regrettable** (11) | which must be regretted, unfortunate |
| **relationship** (3) | connection |
| **remainder** (9) | the rest, the amount left |
| **renowned** (19) | widely known and appreciated |
| **replacement** (7) | substituting perfect goods for defective ones |
| **replacement staff** (17) | someone taking the place of a person who has left |
| **reputable** (15) | well spoken of |
| **request** (9) | act of asking for something |
| **required** (6) | necessary |
| **requirements** (2) | needs |
| **resources** (19) | the means, ability to do something |
| **responsible for** (16) | in charge of |
| **responsibility** (8) | the duty of looking after something, being in charge of something |
| **revise** (11) | to change because of more information |
| **rustic** (5) | simple, as if from the country |

## S

| | |
|---|---|
| **sacking** (5) | strong cloth used for making sacks |

| | |
|---|---|
| **sanding** (4) | making something smooth by rubbing |
| **scales** (3) | a weighing machine |
| **schedule** (1) | a timetable of things to be done |
| **scope** (14) | possibility of selling |
| **scratch** (8) | to mark a surface with something pointed |
| **selection** (14) | a choice, variety |
| **settle** (9) | to pay |
| **settlement** (9) | payment of money for a bill |
| **shawl** (5) | a piece of cloth worn over the head and shoulders |
| **shed** (7) | a wooden building used for storing things, often in a garden |
| **shelf** (7) | a flat piece of wood against a wall for putting things on |
| **shipment** (3) | sending |
| **shortly** (6) | soon |
| **shuttle** (20) | a transport service going to and from a place regularly |
| **software** (1) | disks and programs that make a computer work |
| **sole** (14) | only |
| **solid** (7) | not liquid or gas |
| **standard** (7) | something accepted as a measure of quality |
| **stoppage** (9) | the situation when work has stopped |
| **strap** (3) | a strong, narrow band of material, leather or rope |
| **strapping** (5) | metal bands |
| **strike** (9) | time when work stops because of a disagreement |
| **striped** (4) | patterned with bands of different colour |
| **stipulate** (11) | to demand as a condition |
| **sufficient** (11) | enough |
| **suitability** (16) | fitness for something |
| **suite** (20) | a set of rooms in a hotel |
| **supervisory** (16) | as a person in charge |
| **supplementary** (2) | additional |
| **sympathetically** (16) | agreeing with the feelings of others |

T

| | |
|---|---|
| **tally** (6) | to match |
| **tarpaulin** (4) | a heavy, waterproof cover |
| **temporary** (9) | lasting only for a short time |
| **testimonial** (16) | letter giving details of a person's character and ability |
| **thoroughly** (16) | completely |
| **thriving** (16) | successful |
| **throughout** (15) | in every part of |
| **tradition** (19) | opinions, customs and beliefs that have existed for a long time |
| **transfer** (9) | to move something to another place |
| **tray** (2) | flat piece of metal used for carrying things |
| **trial order** (6) | small order from a client who wants to test the product |
| **trustworthy** (18) | worthy of trust, dependable |
| **tub** (5) | round container |

## U

| | |
|---|---|
| **underwriter** (13) | someone who issues an insurance policy |
| **unfastened** (8) | not joined or fixed to something, not secure |
| **urgent** (9) | needing to be dealt with quickly |
| **utmost** (8) | the most, the greatest |

## V

| | |
|---|---|
| **valve** (3) | a door in a pipe which controls the flow of air or liquid |
| **variety** (14) | different sorts |
| **vary** (14) | to make different |
| **verify** (7) | to make sure of |
| **vet** (16) | to examine carefully for correctness |
| **voucher** (17) | a ticket that may be used instead money |

## W

| | |
|---|---|
| **warehouse** (5) | a building for storing things before they are sold |
| **wholesale** (16) | the business of selling goods in large quantities to shopkeepers |
| **windcheater** (6) | a thick, warm jacket |